THE PELICAN SHAKESPEARE

GENERAL EDITOR ALFRED HARBAGE

A MIDSUMMER NIGHT'S

DREAM

WILLIAM SHAKESPEARE

A MIDSUMMER NIGHT'S DREAM

EDITED BY MADELEINE DORAN

PENGUIN BOOKS

BALTIMORE · MARYLAND

First published in *The Pelican Shakespeare* 1959
This revised edition first published 1971 by
Penguin Books Inc.
7110 Ambassador Road, Baltimore, Maryland 21207

Printed in the United States of America

CONTENTS

PUBLISHER'S NOTE

Soon after the thirty-eight volumes forming *The Pelican Shakespeare* had been published, they were brought together in *The Complete Pelican Shakespeare*. The editorial revisions and new textual features are explained in detail in the General Editor's Preface to the one-volume edition. They have all been incorporated in the present volume. The following should be mentioned in particular:

The lines are not numbered in arbitrary units. Instead all lines are numbered which contain a word, phrase, or allusion explained in the glossarial notes. In the occasional instances where there is a long stretch of unannotated text, certain lines are numbered in italics to serve the conventional reference purpose.

The intrusive and often inaccurate place-headings inserted by early editors are omitted (as is becoming standard practise), but for the convenience of those who miss them, an indication of locale now appears as first item in the annotation of each scene.

In the interest of both elegance and utility, each speech-prefix is set in a separate line when the speaker's lines are in verse, except when these words form the second half of a pentameter line. Thus the verse form of the speech is kept visually intact, and turned-over lines are avoided. What is printed as verse and what is printed as prose has, in general, the authority of the original texts. Departures from the original texts in this regard have only the authority of editorial tradition and the judgment of the Pelican editors; and, in a few instances, are admittedly arbitrary.

SHAKESPEARE AND
HIS STAGE

William Shakespeare was christened in Holy Trinity Church, Stratford-upon-Avon, April 26, 1564. His birth is traditionally assigned to April 23. He was the eldest of four boys and two girls who survived infancy in the family of John Shakespeare, glover and trader of Henley Street, and his wife Mary Arden, daughter of a small landowner of Wilmcote. In 1568 John was elected Bailiff (equivalent to Mayor) of Stratford, having already filled the minor municipal offices. The town maintained for the sons of the burgesses a free school, taught by a university graduate and offering preparation in Latin sufficient for university entrance; its early registers are lost, but there can be little doubt that Shakespeare received the formal part of his education in this school.

On November 27, 1582, a license was issued for the marriage of William Shakespeare (aged eighteen) and Ann Hathaway (aged twenty-six), and on May 26, 1583, their child Susanna was christened in Holy Trinity Church. The inference that the marriage was forced upon the youth is natural but not inevitable; betrothal was legally binding at the time, and was sometimes regarded as conferring conjugal rights. Two additional children of the marriage, the twins Hamnet and Judith, were christened on February 2, 1585. Meanwhile the prosperity of the elder Shakespeares had declined, and William was impelled to seek a career outside Stratford.

The tradition that he spent some time as a country

7

teacher is old but unverifiable. Because of the absence of records his early twenties are called the "lost years," and only one thing about them is certain – that at least some of these years were spent in winning a place in the acting profession. He may have begun as a provincial trouper, but by 1592 he was established in London and prominent enough to be attacked. In a pamphlet of that year, *Groats-worth of Wit*, the ailing Robert Greene complained of the neglect which university writers like himself had suffered from actors, one of whom was daring to set up as a playwright:

. . . an vpstart Crow, beautified with our feathers, that with his *Tygers hart wrapt in a Players hyde,* supposes he is as well able to bombast out a blanke verse as the best of you: and beeing an absolute *Iohannes fac totum,* is in his owne conceit the onely Shake-scene in a countrey.

The pun on his name, and the parody of his line "O tiger's heart wrapped in a woman's hide" (*3 Henry VI*), pointed clearly to Shakespeare. Some of his admirers protested, and Henry Chettle, the editor of Greene's pamphlet, saw fit to apologize:

. . . I am as sory as if the originall fault had beene my fault, because my selfe haue seene his demeanor no lesse ciuill than he excelent in the qualitie he professes: Besides, diuers of worship haue reported his vprightnes of dealing, which argues his honesty, and his facetious grace in writting, that approoues his Art. (Prefatory epistle, *Kind-Harts Dreame*)

The plague closed the London theatres for many months in 1592–94, denying the actors their livelihood. To this period belong Shakespeare's two narrative poems, *Venus and Adonis* and *The Rape of Lucrece*, both dedicated to the Earl of Southampton. No doubt the poet was rewarded with a gift of money as usual in such cases, but he did no further dedicating and we have no reliable information on whether Southampton, or anyone else, became his regular patron. His sonnets, first mentioned in 1598 and published without his consent in 1609, are intimate without being explicitly autobiographical. They seem to commemorate the poet's friendship with an idealized youth, rivalry with a more favored poet, and love affair with a dark mistress; and his bitterness when the mistress betrays him in conjunction with the friend; but it is difficult to decide precisely what the "story" is, impossible to decide whether it is fictional or true. The true distinction of the sonnets, at least of those not purely conventional, rests in the universality of the thoughts and moods they express, and in their poignancy and beauty.

In 1594 was formed the theatrical company known until 1603 as the Lord Chamberlain's men, thereafter as the King's men. Its original membership included, besides Shakespeare, the beloved clown Will Kempe and the famous actor Richard Burbage. The company acted in various London theatres and even toured the provinces, but it is chiefly associated in our minds with the Globe Theatre built on the south bank of the Thames in 1599. Shakespeare was an actor and joint owner of this company (and its Globe) through the remainder of his creative years. His plays, written at the average rate of two a year, together with Burbage's acting won it its place of leadership among the London companies.

Individual plays began to appear in print, in editions both honest and piratical, and the publishers became increasingly aware of the value of Shakespeare's name on the title pages. As early as 1598 he was hailed as the leading English dramatist in the *Palladis Tamia* of Francis Meres:

As *Plautus* and *Seneca* are accounted the best for Comedy and Tragedy among the Latines, so *Shakespeare* among the English is the most excellent in both kinds for the stage: for Comedy, witnes his *Gentlemen of Verona*, his *Errors*, his *Loue labors lost*, his *Loue labours wonne* [at one time in print but no longer extant, at least under this title], his *Midsummers night dream*, & his *Merchant of Venice*; for Tragedy, his *Richard the 2*, *Richard the 3*, *Henry the 4*, *King Iohn*, *Titus Andronicus*, and his *Romeo and Iuliet*.

The note is valuable both in indicating Shakespeare's prestige and in helping us to establish a chronology. In the second half of his writing career, history plays gave place to the great tragedies; and farces and light comedies gave place to the problem plays and symbolic romances. In 1623, seven years after his death, his former fellow-actors, John Heminge and Henry Condell, cooperated with a group of London printers in bringing out his plays in collected form. The volume is generally known as the First Folio.

Shakespeare had never severed his relations with Stratford. His wife and children may sometimes have shared his London lodgings, but their home was Stratford. His son Hamnet was buried there in 1596, and his daughters Susanna and Judith were married there in 1607 and 1616 respectively. (His father, for whom he had secured a coat of arms and thus the privilege of writing himself gentleman, died in 1601, his mother in 1608.) His considerable earnings in London, as actor-sharer, part owner of the Globe, and playwright, were invested chiefly in Stratford property. In 1597 he purchased for £60 New Place, one of the two most imposing residences in the town. A number of other business transactions, as well as minor episodes in his career, have left documentary records. By 1611 he was in a position to retire, and he seems gradually to have withdrawn from theatrical activity in order to live in Stratford. In March, 1616, he made a will, leaving token bequests to Burbage, Heminge, and Condell, but the bulk of his estate to his family. The most famous feature of the will, the bequest of the second-best bed to his wife, reveals nothing about Shakespeare's marriage; the quaintness of the provision seems commonplace to those familiar with ancient testaments. Shakespeare died April 23, 1616, and was buried in the Stratford church where he had been christened. Within seven years a monument was erected to his memory on the north wall of the chancel. Its portrait bust and the Droeshout engraving on the title page of the First Folio provide the only likenesses with an established claim to authenticity. The best verbal vignette was written by his rival Ben Jonson, the more impressive for being imbedded in a context mainly critical :

... I loved the man, and doe honour his memory (on this side idolatry) as much as any. Hee was indeed honest, and of an open and free nature: had an excellent Phantsie, brave notions, and gentle expressions.... (*Timber or Discoveries,* ca. 1623–30)

*

The reader of Shakespeare's plays is aided by a general knowledge of the way in which they were staged. The King's men acquired a roofed and artificially lighted theatre only toward the close of Shakespeare's career, and then only for winter use. Nearly all his plays were designed for performance in such structures as the Globe – a three-tiered amphitheatre with a large rectangular platform extending to the center of its yard. The plays were staged by daylight, by large casts brilliantly costumed, but with only a minimum of properties, without scenery, and quite possibly without intermissions. There was a rear stage gallery for action "above," and a curtained rear recess for "discoveries" and other special effects, but by far the major portion of any play was enacted upon the projecting platform, with episode following episode in swift succession, and with shifts of time and place signaled the audience only by the momentary clearing of the stage between the episodes. Information about the identity of the characters and, when necessary, about the time and place of the action was incorporated in the dialogue. No place-headings have been inserted in the present editions ; these are apt to obscure the original fluidity of structure, with the emphasis upon action and speech rather than scenic background. (Indications of place are supplied in the footnotes.) The acting, including that of the youthful apprentices to the profession who performed the parts of women, was highly skillful, with a premium placed upon grace of gesture and beauty of diction. The audiences, a cross section of the general public, commonly numbered a thousand, sometimes more than two thousand. Judged by the type of plays they applauded, these audiences were not only large but also perceptive.

THE TEXTS OF THE PLAYS

About half of Shakespeare's plays appeared in print for the first time in the folio volume of 1623. The others had been published individually, usually in quarto volumes, during his lifetime or in the six years following his death. The copy used by the printers of the quartos varied greatly in merit, sometimes representing Shakespeare's true text, sometimes only a debased version of that text. The copy used by the printers of the folio also varied in merit, but was chosen with care. Since it consisted of the best available manuscripts, or the more acceptable quartos (although frequently in editions other than the first), or of quartos corrected by reference to manuscripts, we have good or reasonably good texts of most of the thirty-seven plays.

In the present series, the plays have been newly edited from quarto or folio texts, depending, when a choice offered, upon which is now regarded by bibliographical specialists as the more authoritative. The ideal has been to reproduce the chosen texts with as few alterations as possible, beyond occasional relineation, expansion of abbreviations, and modernization of punctuation and spelling. Emendation is held to a minimum, and such material as has been added, in the way of stage directions and lines supplied by an alternative text, has been enclosed in square brackets.

None of the plays printed in Shakespeare's lifetime were divided into acts and scenes, and the inference is that the author's own manuscripts were not so divided. In the folio collection, some of the plays remained undivided, some were divided into acts, and some were divided into acts and scenes. During the eighteenth century all of the plays were divided into acts and scenes, and in the Cambridge edition of the mid-nineteenth century, from which the influential Globe text derived, this division was more or less regularized and the lines were numbered. Many useful works of reference employ the act–scene–line apparatus thus established.

Since this act–scene division is obviously convenient, but is of very dubious authority so far as Shakespeare's own structural principles are concerned, or the original manner of staging his plays, a problem is presented to modern editors. In the present series the act–scene division is retained marginally, and may be viewed as a reference aid like the line numbering. A star marks the points of division when these points have been determined by a cleared stage indicating a shift of time and place in the action of the play, or when no harm results from the editorial assumption that there is such a shift. However, at those points where the established division is clearly misleading – that is, where continuous action has been split up into separate "scenes" – the star is omitted and the distortion corrected. This mechanical expedient seemed the best means of combining utility and accuracy.

THE GENERAL EDITOR

INTRODUCTION

A Midsummer Night's Dream is one of Shakespeare's happiest comedies. It is called a dream because the improbable events of the story seem to the participants when they are over like something dreamed, true yet not true – such a dream of crossed loves, futile quarrels, and frustrated searches, of fairy spells and strange transformations as belongs to Midsummer Eve, June 23, a night when men are proverbially subject to fairy tricks and queer fancies. "Methought I was, and methought I had – But man is but a patched fool if he will offer to say what methought I had." Yet the play is not just a fairy tale, for everyone knows that love is blind, and that mortals possessed with it readily make delightful fools of themselves. The characters in the play are only visited with the midsummer madness common to lovers in or out of fairy-haunted woods.

The absurd dream, however, is followed by a "solemnity," a happy but serious celebration of a multiple wedding. Marriage, of course, is the expected ending of a comedy of love; but the formality of these nuptials and the presence of the fairies to sing an epithalamium and to bless the bride-beds suggest that the play may have been written as an entertainment for a great wedding, just as Quince's play was written for the wedding festival of Theseus and Hippolyta. Attempts have been made to find such a wedding of a suitable date. Among the several noble weddings proposed, ranging from 1591 to 1598, the one most favored is that of William Stanley, Earl of Derby (whose father and whose brother had been patrons of Shakespeare's company of actors), to Elizabeth Vere, daughter of the Earl of Oxford, on January 26, 1595; it was performed at Greenwich Palace and Queen Elizabeth may have attended it. The manifest compliment to the Queen in Oberon's lines on "the imperial vot'ress" in Act II, scene i, would have been appropriate to an occasion when she was present. The few suspected topical allusions in the play appear to indicate a similar date. The most important one is the unseasonable weather described in II, i, 81–117, which would fit any one of the three years 1594–96 but especially the cold and sodden summer of 1594. The best indication of approximate date lies in the style. The blank verse shows the easy handling Shakespeare had attained after writing plays for six or seven years, without showing the bolder freedom and more complex rhythms of later years. Composition in 1594 or 1595 would make the play fall at the end of Shakespeare's first years of experiment with drama, during which time he learned to harness to the needs of a play his schoolboy training in rhetoric, his fondness for playing with words, metres, and rhymes, his delight in poetry for its own sake. Like *Richard II* and *Romeo and Juliet*, both probably to be dated about 1595, *A Midsummer Night's Dream* is full of lyricism, not subdued, yet fully controlled for a dramatic purpose. In *Richard II*, the hero's living in a world of poetic images is made the key to his psychological tragedy ; in *Romeo and Juliet*, in which the intense and tragic love of two very young people is enacted against a background of family feud, setting and poetry are made to sustain and illuminate the action. So they are in *A Midsummer Night's Dream*. The poetry creates the wood, the moonlight, and the fairies, and it is in the wood, under fairy spells, that all the fantastic events of the night take place.

Whether or not there was a private occasion for the play, we know by the statement on the title page of the first edition, a quarto printed in 1600, that it was "sundry times publicly acted" by the Lord Chamberlain's servants, that is, by Shakespeare's company. Certain irregularities in the 1600 text and certain features of the play, notably inconsistencies in the time scheme (both in the duration of the action and in the state of the moon, which is dark when the play opens but most effectively shining the following night), suggest that the play may have undergone some rewriting, but when and how much we have no way of knowing. If Shakespeare revised the play, he did it skillfully enough not to destroy its unity. Inconsistencies in the calendar apart, the play is all of a piece, with its several actions, its fantasy and its low comedy, its variety of styles for different situations and characters, all contributing to the whole design.

That design falls into four component groups of characters and their actions: Theseus and Hippolyta, whose court in Athens furnishes a frame setting for the main plot and whose expected wedding makes an occasion for the play; the four young lovers, who run away from Athens and whose misadventures in the wood make up the principal action (on the eve of May Day, by the way, rather than on the eve of Midsummer Night, as we might expect); the fairies in the wood, who are having troubles of their own, but who, more or less by the way, intervene in the lovers' affairs to make them first worse, then better; and the "hempen homespuns," a group of Athenian craftsmen who come into the wood to rehearse a little play they hope to present at court for the wedding festivities, and who, in an unexpected way, also fall foul of the fairies. The fairies also come to court at the end to bring their blessings to the three newly wedded couples. And so each of the plots and groups of characters touches one of the others at some point.

The court, where the action begins and ends, is elegant, ceremonious, a scene "with pomp, with triumph, and with revelling." The blank verse generally spoken there helps to set off the courtly background, with its greater formality and decorum, from the comic adventures of the lovers. Duke Theseus is slightly, but adequately, sketched as a hero, a huntsman, and a sage prince. He is a strong, sensible, kind ruler, not particularly imaginative, and skeptical of fantasy, whether in lovers' brains or in poets'. To make him so, in this play of all others, is a nice touch of Shakespearean irony. The court, for all its gaiety, is the stable world of common sense and social order.

The desperate alternatives Theseus lays before Hermia – either to marry Demetrius, the man of her father's choice, or to betake herself to a cloister – drive her and Lysander into the woods, with Demetrius hot after them and Helena close behind. This device of taking his characters away from court and city into a freer, half fairy-tale world (a device he was to employ again in *As You Like It*, *The Winter's Tale*, and *The Tempest*) Shakespeare first fully discovered in *A Midsummer Night's Dream*. Credibility may be suspended for the sake of fun, of poetry, and of comic vision. By making the fairies responsible for the young men's change of heart, he plays lightly on his comic theme, that love is hardly a rational state; at the same time he saves his lovers from such harsh judgments of fickleness as readers are inclined to visit on Proteus in the earlier comedy of *The Two Gentlemen of Verona*. For one scarcely remembers, after such a night of errors, that Demetrius first altered his affections without the aid of the love-juice; his breach of faith seems like part of the dream. When the sick fancy is cured, the heart returns to its true-love. The plotting of the complications is neat. With Puck's applications of the juice and of its antidote, the young men's changes of heart follow a simple diagrammatic scheme: before the action of the play starts, each one loved his own girl; when it begins both love Hermia, then each loves the wrong girl, then both love Helena; finally, each loves the right girl again. As is fitting to such a state of things, neither lover can be much distinguished from the other, being both just infatuated young men, and as violently sure there was never anyone like Helena one minute as they had been sure the moment before there was never anyone like Hermia. The girls have more personality and individuality. Hermia is little and dark and a spitfire; Helena is tall and blonde and weepy, making much of her feminine woes and helplessness, yet quite as dogged in pursuit of her man as Hermia. The verse of the lovers varies between the blank verse they speak with the court group or when showing some elevation of feeling (as in Helena's lovely lines on her childhood friendship with Hermia) and the pentameter couplets and cross-rhymes they speak when they are quarrelling or making love. These rhyming passages, with their slight artificiality and lightness of touch, heighten the comedy.

The third element in the play, the fairy world, furnishes a slight secondary plot, as well as the machinery for the confusion of the main plot. The family quarrel of Titania and Oberon over the changeling boy is invented, perhaps, simply to bring the love-juice into the play. But, characteristically, Shakespeare gives this minor action depth and atmosphere, with glimpses of an Indian princess on a faraway shore and of Theseus' abandoned loves, hence endowing it with a vitality of its own. The primary purpose of the magic herbs – one to blind the sight with fancied love, the other to cure it – appears, of course, to be to further Oberon's revenge on Titania. But by his casual order to Puck to anoint the eyes of a disdainful youth in Athenian garments, the herbs are brought most naturally into the main plot, where Shakespeare uses them ingeniously both to tie and to untie the knot of his complication. The fairies appear to be very busy about mortal affairs, but their interventions are, on the whole, well intended. Though they are abroad at night, they are not powers of darkness. If their mischief or their spite sometimes brings vexations, their goodwill brings blessings. They are, in short, the minor powers of the unseen world that make the little things of daily life go right or wrong. Puck, besides, is the comic chorus of the play, its spirit of fun: "Lord, what fools these mortals be!" One would think he had had nothing to do with their foolishness.

Oberon and Titania, in their beauty, their rule over fairyland and a courtly train, their travelling of great distances, their powers of enchantment, and their limited influence over human affairs, are like "the Faery" of late medieval tales and ballads, known to everybody; sometimes, as well, of romances, which, extended and debased, had become the favorite popular reading of the sixteenth century. But Robin Goodfellow is a native country imp of folk superstition, a "puck," an ugly, merry, mischievous hobgoblin. His name "Goodfellow" is less a surname than a propitiatory epithet, for he has it in his power to annoy in the way that the modern gremlins have; but he is friendly enough if well treated. Left a bowl of milk on a tidy hearth, he will make the household chores go right; neglected, he will put everything at sixes and sevens. In associating "literary" with folk fairies Shakespeare was not doing anything novel or incongruous, for fairy lore in his day was already an inextricable mixture of literary tradition (both medieval and classical), folk belief, religious teaching (which associated the fairies with evil spirits), and poetic invention. Like other poets before him, Shakespeare enriched the blend, and added something unusual; that is, the miniature size of the fairies, who were commonly not smaller than children and were often the size of adults. But since the parts of Shakespeare's fairies must have been taken on the stage by boys old enough to play them, their diminutiveness is mainly for poetic effect (as in Mercutio's Queen Mab speech in *Romeo and Juliet*), an imaginative suggestion of elegance and daintiness. It is the poetry, after all, which creates the enchantment of the wood. Titania and Oberon, in keeping with decorum, generally speak in blank verse, like the characters in the human court; their verse, too, carries the weight of the imaginative description of the fairy world. But Oberon's description of Titania's bower and his instructions to Puck are given special emphasis by being rhymed; and his and Puck's spells are pronounced in verse of shorter metre, usually octosyllabic, or four-stress, lines rhyming alternately or in couplets. The little fairies sing in tripping measures with shorter lines.

The fourth element in the play, the group of "mechanicals," is brought into it for the salt of low comedy. But they, too, coming into the wood to rehearse their interlude, are led naturally into the action. Partly through the accident of their choosing a grassy plot near Titania's bower, partly through Puck's mischief, Bottom, with his "fair large ears," becomes the object of the dainty queen's deluded fancy. So the theme of love-blindness is played in another key, and given ludicrous emphasis. Bottom's part, probably performed by Will Kempe, the famous comedian of Shakespeare's company, is in the same line of clowns as Launce in *The Two Gentlemen* and Dogberry in *Much Ado about Nothing*. Like Dogberry, Bottom is wonderfully self-sufficient. His aplomb is quite undisturbed by the refinements of Titania's court and by the love of the Fairy Queen. Bottom and his friends speak in prose, not primarily because of their social class, but in order to set off the tone of their comedy from the rest of the play. The courtiers speak in prose, too, when they are joking at the performance of the interlude.

That little play, which Bottom and his friends so much admire, is written partly in pentameter couplets, partly in a variation of the common ballad stanza. The ballad metre, in a monotonous jog-trot line of fourteen syllables known as the "fourteener" (Quince's "eight and six"), had been common in stage-plays written before the development of blank verse. The language of the interlude is only a slightly exaggerated parody of the horrendous vocabulary and excessive alliteration to be found in early translations of Seneca's tragedies. The subject of the play, the story of

Pyramus and Thisbe, was (like the story of Romeo and Juliet, its offshoot) a perennial tale of faithful and unfortunate love, and was well worn through centuries of retelling. The time and the scene of it, ancient Babylon, would seem fitting to the court of Theseus. For his version of the tale Shakespeare went directly to the first telling of it in his favorite classical book, the *Metamorphoses* of Ovid. But several versions, written in clumsy verse and in exaggerated rhetorical style, had been published during Shakespeare's youth in anthologies of verse; they give point to his outrageous parody. Narrative poems, too, on other famous legendary lovers (like Marlowe's *Hero and Leander*) were fashionable in the early nineties.

This admixture, in *A Midsummer Night's Dream*, of romantic adventure, sympathetic sentiment, fantasy, burlesque, and earthy comedy, and of characters of high and low degree, was agreeable to English taste and to Shakespeare's genius. It was his first masterpiece in this kind of comedy that we call romantic, a kind he continued to develop and to vary for the rest of his life. Compared with the greater comedies to follow, richer in portrayal of character and deeper in sympathy, and compared especially with his other fairy-tale play, *The Tempest*, which is the product of his ripest wisdom and of his maturest art, *A Midsummer Night's Dream* may seem a pretty toy. But the lesser thing it does it does to perfection. It is a little triumph – one of the earliest of Shakespeare's plays in which things so disparate and so various are gathered up into a single whole.

There is another kind of mixture in this play, also successfully achieved; that is the blending of material from different sources, classical, medieval, and contemporary, literary and popular. The lovers' plot appears to have no particular source (rather surprisingly, since there was no prejudice in Shakespeare's time against an author's taking a good story where he found it; what he did with it was what counted). But to enrich and complicate the core

of his play, Shakespeare drew on a memory well stored
with his varied reading and with the fairy lore he had ab-
sorbed in childhood. For the legend of Theseus he went to
Chaucer's *Knight's Tale* and perhaps his *Legend of Good
Women*, to Plutarch's *Lives* in Thomas North's translation
(1579), and to Ovid's *Metamorphoses*; for the name of
Oberon, probably to the French romance of *Huon of Bor-
deaux* (in English by about 1540), where Oberon is the
dwarf King of the Faery, or to *The Faerie Queene*, where
he is an Elfin prince, father of Gloriana, Spenser's "Faerie
Queene" (II, i, 8; II, x, 75, 76); for the name of Titania,
to the *Metamorphoses*, where it is used as an epithet both of
Diana (III, 173) and of Circe the enchantress (XIV, 14, 382,
438), descendants of the Titans; for Bottom's transformation, possibly, but not necessarily, to Apuleius' *Golden
Ass* (translated by William Adlington, 1566); for the
Pyramus and Thisbe story and much besides, to the *Metamorphoses* (IV, 55–166), both in a Latin edition and in
Arthur Golding's many-times-printed English translation.
Shakespeare fancied a metamorphosis of the pansy in
playful Ovidian spirit, and allusions to other names and
legends he wove delicately but persistently into the poetic
texture of the play. He thus took some pains, it would
appear, to give his comedy a "classical" flavor in keeping
with the Athenian setting. But it is classical in the Renaissance manner. The ancient past is not, in Shakespeare and
his contemporaries, a cold, reconstructed museum piece
of archaeologically correct figures. Having been part of a
continuous living tradition through intervening centuries,
it is easily caught up into the present, for new meanings
and purposes, when it is once again sought as a fresh
source. In such art, anachronism is unobtrusive, because
it has no absolute standard to falsify; it is, moreover,
necessary. Shakespeare's Theseus has something in him
of the legendary hero who rivalled Hercules in his exploits, of Plutarch's wise statesman, and of Chaucer's
chivalric duke, who went a-hunting with horn and hounds

in an English wood on a May morning, and who conquered and wedded "the queene Ipolita,"

> And broghte her hoom with him in his contree,
> With muchel glorie and greet solempnitee.

All this without jar, for he is a new character in his own right.

The play in one form or another has had a lively but not very satisfactory acting history. Some time before the printing of the folio in 1623 it may have been arranged for a newer style of performance, with act pauses; some slight changes were made in the assignment of minor parts. There are several references to performances in the early seventeenth century, but to only one, which Pepys found insipid and ridiculous, in the Restoration. Sufficient for performance as the play is, producers have seldom until recent times – and not always then – been willing to let it take care of itself. During the Restoration, the eighteenth century, and the early part of the nineteenth, it underwent two opposite kinds of mangling – one in the direction of burlesque, with action reduced to Bottom's transformation and to the craftsmen's rehearsal and performance of *Pyramus and Thisbe*; the other in the direction of opera, or pseudo-opera, with the low comedy drastically cut or omitted altogether, the lovers' and fairies' dialogue cut, but their parts expanded with songs, and the whole filled out with extraneous shows and dances. The earliest known example of the former kind of adaptation is a "droll" printed in 1661, *The Merry Conceited Humours of Bottom the Weaver*. (The title would have been appropriate to many later cut versions of the play.) The first and most famous of a long line of operatic adaptations was *The Fairy Queen* in 1692, for which Purcell wrote the music. (This has been successfully revived in our time, for the sake of the music.) Every act was supplied with ingenious and irrelevant shows; the one in Act V included a duet by a Chinese man and woman, a chorus of "Chineses," a

dance of monkeys, and a "Grand Dance of 24 Chinese."
Even the version of the play attributed to Garrick and
performed in 1755, with a prologue spoken by him, was
operatic. It was the mid-nineteenth century before the
play was again seen on the English stage as a spoken play
wholly in Shakespeare's words. Even during that century
it was often severely cut and arranged. It has taken the
great influence of William Poel and Harley Granville-
Barker early in our own century to teach directors and
producers that Shakespeare wrote his plays with the
theatre in mind from the start and that to cut them up and
pull them about is to lose the very things that make them
most successful on the stage.

The style of the Victorian and Edwardian periods called
for elaborate pictorial settings, even, in Herbert Beerbohm
Tree's magnificent production in 1911, to the introduction of live rabbits in the wood. A return to Shakespeare's
more fluid principles of staging, with nearly continuous
action, with increased pace in the speaking, and with
scenery and costume more symbolic and less literal, was
made in Granville-Barker's production at the Savoy in
1914.

Among other productions notable for various reasons
have been Ludwig Tieck's German version in Berlin in
1827, for which Mendelssohn wrote his still popular musical setting; Samuel Phelps's charming production at
Sadler's Wells in 1853, with himself as Bottom; and
Charles Kean's production in 1856, in which Ellen Terry
at the age of eight played Puck. Contemporary productions are often boldly experimental. The play is a popular
one among the various repertory and festival companies,
and of course in any year it may be seen in school and
college auditoriums – often very well played, too. Hap-
pily, its charm survives nearly any kind of treatment.

University of Wisconsin   MADELEINE DORAN

NOTE ON THE TEXT

The present edition follows the text of the first quarto (1600), which was probably printed from Shakespeare's own revised draft of the play. It is well printed as play quartos go, but it contains some troublesome misreadings of the manuscript as well as minor compositors' slips. This text was reprinted in 1619 in a second quarto falsely dated 1600, and the latter, altered by reference to theatrical manuscript, was used as copy by the printers of the folio of 1623. (Comment upon the interrelation of these early texts is provided in an appended note.) The text of the quartos is not divided into acts and scenes. That of the folio is divided into acts but not into scenes. The acts were divided into scenes by later editors, and this familiar division is provided marginally for reference in the present edition.

A MIDSUMMER
NIGHT'S
DREAM

Theseus, Duke of Athens
Egeus, father to Hermia
Lysander, beloved of Hermia
Demetrius, suitor to Hermia, approved by Egeus
Philostrate, Master of the Revels to Theseus
Peter Quince, a carpenter ; Prologue in the interlude
Nick Bottom, a weaver ; Pyramus in the same
Francis Flute, a bellows-mender ; Thisby in the same
Tom Snout, a tinker ; Wall in the same
Snug, a joiner ; Lion in the same
Robin Starveling, a tailor ; Moonshine in the same
Hippolyta, Queen of the Amazons, betrothed to Theseus
Hermia, daughter to Egeus, in love with Lysander
Helena, in love with Demetrius
Oberon, King of the Fairies
Titania, Queen of the Fairies
Puck, or Robin Goodfellow
Peaseblossom
Cobweb
} *fairies*
Moth
Mustardseed
Other Fairies attending Oberon and Titania.
  Attendants on Theseus and Hippolyta.

Scene : *Athens, and a wood near by*]

A MIDSUMMER
NIGHT'S
DREAM

Enter Theseus, Hippolyta, [Philostrate,] with others. I, i

THESEUS

Now, fair Hippolyta, our nuptial hour
Draws on apace. Four happy days bring in
Another moon; but O, methinks, how slow
This old moon wanes! She lingers my desires,
Like to a stepdame or a dowager,
Long withering out a young man's revenue.

HIPPOLYTA

Four days will quickly steep themselves in night,
Four nights will quickly dream away the time;
And then the moon, like to a silver bow
New-bent in heaven, shall behold the night
Of our solemnities.

THESEUS   Go, Philostrate,
Stir up the Athenian youth to merriments,
Awake the pert and nimble spirit of mirth,
Turn melancholy forth to funerals;
The pale companion is not for our pomp.   15

                    [Exit Philostrate.]

Hippolyta, I wooed thee with my sword,   16
And won thy love doing thee injuries;
But I will wed thee in another key,

I, i The palace of the Duke   **15** *companion* fellow; *pomp* splendid ceremony,
'solemn sight' (Cawdrey's dictionary, 1604)   **16** *Hippolyta . . . sword*
(according to Chaucer and to one story in Plutarch, Theseus had taken
Hippolyta captive when he conquered the Amazons)

29

19   With pomp, with triumph, and with revelling.

Enter Egeus and his daughter Hermia, and Lysander and Demetrius.

EGEUS

Happy be Theseus, our renownèd Duke.

THESEUS

21   Thanks, good Egeus. What's the news with thee?

EGEUS

Full of vexation come I, with complaint
Against my child, my daughter Hermia.
Stand forth, Demetrius. My noble lord,
This man hath my consent to marry her.
Stand forth, Lysander. And, my gracious Duke,

27   This man hath bewitched the bosom of my child.
Thou, thou, Lysander, thou hast given her rhymes
And interchanged love tokens with my child;
Thou hast by moonlight at her window sung
With feigning voice verses of feigning love,

32   And stol'n the impression of her fantasy

33   With bracelets of thy hair, rings, gauds, conceits,

34   Knacks, trifles, nosegays, sweetmeats – messengers
Of strong prevailment in unhardened youth.

36   With cunning hast thou filched my daughter's heart,
Turned her obedience (which is due to me)
To stubborn harshness. And, my gracious Duke,
Be it so she will not here before your Grace
Consent to marry with Demetrius,
I beg the ancient privilege of Athens:
As she is mine, I may dispose of her,
Which shall be either to this gentleman
Or to her death, according to our law

45   Immediately provided in that case.

19 *with triumph* (1) magnificently, with public festivities, (2) victoriously   **21** *Egeus* (pronounced *E-gè-us*)   **27** *bewitched* (with a literal as well as a metaphorical suggestion)   **32** *stol'n . . . fantasy* i.e. stealthily imprinted thine image upon her fancy   **33** *gauds* trinkets; *conceits* fanciful trifles   **34** *Knacks* knickknacks   **36** *cunning* expert knowledge (cf. l. 27)   **45** *Immediately* expressly

THESEUS

    What say you, Hermia? Be advised, fair maid.
    To you your father should be as a god,
    One that composed your beauties; yea, and one
    To whom you are but as a form in wax,
    By him imprinted, and within his power
    To leave the figure, or disfigure it.   51
    Demetrius is a worthy gentleman.   52

HERMIA

    So is Lysander.

THESEUS   In himself he is;
    But in this kind, wanting your father's voice,   54
    The other must be held the worthier.

HERMIA

    I would my father looked but with my eyes.

THESEUS

    Rather your eyes must with his judgment look.

HERMIA

    I do entreat your Grace to pardon me.
    I know not by what power I am made bold,
    Nor how it may concern my modesty
    In such a presence here to plead my thoughts;
    But I beseech your Grace that I may know
    The worst that may befall me in this case
    If I refuse to wed Demetrius.

THESEUS

    Either to die the death, or to abjure
    For ever the society of men.
    Therefore, fair Hermia, question your desires,
    Know of your youth, examine well your blood,   68
    Whether, if you yield not to your father's choice,
    You can endure the livery of a nun,
    For aye to be in shady cloister mewed,   70
    To live a barren sister all your life,

51 *To leave . . . it* to leave the image as it is, or destroy it   52 *worthy* noble
54 *in this kind* in this respect (as a husband); *voice* consent   68 *blood*
passions   70 *livery* habit   71 *mewed* caged

31

73 Chanting faint hymns to the cold fruitless moon.
Thrice blessèd they that master so their blood
To undergo such maiden pilgrimage ;
76 But earthlier happy is the rose distilled
Than that which, withering on the virgin thorn,
Grows, lives, and dies in single blessedness.

HERMIA

So will I grow, so live, so die, my lord,
80 Ere I will yield my virgin patent up
Unto his lordship whose unwishèd yoke
My soul consents not to give sovereignty.

THESEUS

Take time to pause ; and by the next new moon –
The sealing day betwixt my love and me
For everlasting bond of fellowship –
Upon that day either prepare to die
For disobedience to your father's will,
Or else to wed Demetrius, as he would,
Or on Diana's altar to protest
For aye austerity and single life.

DEMETRIUS

Relent, sweet Hermia ; and, Lysander, yield
92 Thy crazèd title to my certain right.

it is his right to have her

LYSANDER

You have her father's love, Demetrius ;
Let me have Hermia's: do you marry him.

EGEUS

Scornful Lysander, true, he hath my love,
And what is mine my love shall render him.
And she is mine, and all my right of her
98 I do estate unto Demetrius.

LYSANDER

99 I am, my lord, as well derived as he,

---

73 *Chanting . . . moon* (Hermia would be a votaress of Diana, the virgin goddess)   76 *earthlier happy* (opposed to *blessèd*, l. 74); *distilled* i.e. made into perfume   80 *virgin patent* patent or privilege of virginity   92 *crazèd* cracked, flawed   98 *estate unto* settle upon   99 *well derived* well born

As well possessed ; my love is more than his ;   100
My fortunes every way as fairly ranked   101
(If not with vantage) as Demetrius' ;   102
And (which is more than all these boasts can be)
I am beloved of beauteous Hermia.
Why should not I then prosecute my right ?
Demetrius, I'll avouch it to his head,   106
Made love to Nedar's daughter, Helena,
And won her soul ; and she (sweet lady) dotes,
Devoutly dotes, dotes in idolatry,
Upon this spotted and inconstant man.   110

THESEUS
I must confess that I have heard so much,
And with Demetrius thought to have spoke thereof ;
But, being over-full of self-affairs,
My mind did lose it. But Demetrius, come,
And come, Egeus. You shall go with me ;
I have some private schooling for you both.
For you, fair Hermia, look you arm yourself   117
To fit your fancies to your father's will ;   118
Or else the law of Athens yields you up
(Which by no means we may extenuate)   120
To death, or to a vow of single life.
Come, my Hippolyta. What cheer, my love ?
Demetrius and Egeus, go along.
I must employ you in some business
Against our nuptial and confer with you   125
Of something nearly that concerns yourselves.   126

EGEUS
With duty and desire we follow you.
                    Exeunt [all but Lysander and Hermia].

---

100 *well possessed* rich   **101** *fortunes . . . ranked* both wealth and position as
good   **102** *with vantage* somewhat better   **106** *head* face   **110** *spotted* i.e.
morally spotted, untrustworthy   **117** *look . . . yourself* see that you get
ready   **118** *fancies* love-thoughts ('fancy' means both imagination and
love)   **120** *extenuate* mitigate   **125** *Against* in preparation for   **126** *nearly*
closely (modifies *confer*)

LYSANDER

How now, my love? Why is your cheek so pale?
How chance the roses there do fade so fast?

HERMIA

130 Belike for want of rain, which I could well
131 Beteem them from the tempest of my eyes.

LYSANDER

Ay me! for aught that I could ever read,
Could ever hear by tale or history,
The course of true love never did run smooth;
But either it was different in blood –

HERMIA

O cross! too high to be enthralled to low.

LYSANDER

137 Or else misgraffèd in respect of years –

HERMIA

O spite! too old to be engaged to young.

LYSANDER

139 Or else it stood upon the choice of friends –

HERMIA

O hell! to choose love by another's eyes.

LYSANDER

Or, if there were a sympathy in choice,
War, death, or sickness did lay siege to it,
143 Making it momentany as a sound,
Swift as a shadow, short as any dream,
145 Brief as the lightning in the collied night,
146 That, in a spleen, unfolds both heaven and earth,
And ere a man hath power to say 'Behold!'
The jaws of darkness do devour it up:
So quick bright things come to confusion.

130 *Belike* perhaps 131 *Beteem* allow, afford 137 *misgraffèd* ill-grafted
139 *friends* relatives, parents 143 *momentany* momentary (Latin '*mo-mentaneus*') 145 *collied* murky (literally, blackened with coal-dust)
146 *in a spleen* (1) on a sudden impulse, hence in a flash, (2) in a fit of violent temper

HERMIA

  If then true lovers have been ever crossed,
  It stands as an edict in destiny:
  Then let us teach our trial patience,   152
  Because it is a customary cross,   153
  As due to love as thoughts, and dreams, and sighs,
  Wishes, and tears, poor Fancy's followers.   155

LYSANDER

  A good persuasion. Therefore hear me, Hermia.
  I have a widow aunt, a dowager,
  Of great revenue, and she hath no child.   158
  From Athens is her house remote seven leagues,
  And she respects me as her only son.
  There, gentle Hermia, may I marry thee,
  And to that place the sharp Athenian law
  Cannot pursue us. If thou lovest me then,
  Steal forth thy father's house to-morrow night;
  And in the wood, a league without the town
  (Where I did meet thee once with Helena
  To do observance to a morn of May),
  There will I stay for thee.

HERMIA   My good Lysander,
  I swear to thee by Cupid's strongest bow,
  By his best arrow, with the golden head,   170
  By the simplicity of Venus' doves,   171
  By that which knitteth souls and prospers loves,
  And by that fire which burned the Carthage queen   173
  When the false Troyan under sail was seen,
  By all the vows that ever men have broke
  (In number more than ever women spoke),

---

152 *teach . . . patience* i.e. school ourselves to be patient in this trial 153 *cross* thwarting, vexation 155 *Fancy's* Love's 158 *revenue* (pronounced 'revènue') 170 *best . . . head* (Cupid's sharp golden arrow causes love, his blunt leaden one dislike) 171 *simplicity* guilelessness, sincerity; *Venus' doves* (doves drew Venus' chariot) 173-74 *fire . . . seen* (Dido Queen of Carthage immolated herself on a funeral pyre when the Trojan Aeneas sailed away)

In that same place thou hast appointed me
To-morrow truly will I meet with thee.

LYSANDER

Keep promise, love. Look, here comes Helena.
Enter Helena.

HERMIA

180   God speed fair Helena. Whither away?

HELENA

Call you me fair? That fair again unsay.

182   Demetrius loves your fair. O happy fair!

183   Your eyes are lodestars, and your tongue's sweet air
More tuneable than lark to shepherd's ear
When wheat is green, when hawthorn buds appear.

186   Sickness is catching. O, were favor so,
Yours would I catch, fair Hermia, ere I go;
My ear should catch your voice, my eye your eye,
My tongue should catch your tongue's sweet melody.

190   Were the world mine, Demetrius being bated,

191   The rest I'ld give to be to you translated.

192   O, teach me how you look, and with what art

193   You sway the motion of Demetrius' heart.

HERMIA

I frown upon him; yet he loves me still.

HELENA

O that your frowns would teach my smiles such skill!

HERMIA

I give him curses; yet he gives me love.

HELENA

O that my prayers could such affection move!

HERMIA

The more I hate, the more he follows me.

---

180 *fair* beautiful (blonde only by implication, because a light complexion
was the standard of beauty)   **182** *your fair* your type of beauty (Hermia is
dark; see II, ii, 114 and III, ii, 257); *happy fair* fortunate fair one ('lucky
woman')   **183** *lodestars* guiding stars (like the polestar); *air* music   **186**
favor looks, especially good looks   **190** *bated* excepted   **191** *translated*
transformed   **192** *art* (carries suggestion of magic art; cf. I, i, 27, 36)
193 *motion* impulses, affection

HELENA

The more I love, the more he hateth me.

HERMIA

His folly, Helena, is no fault of mine.

HELENA

None but your beauty. Would that fault were mine!

HERMIA

Take comfort. He no more shall see my face;
Lysander and myself will fly this place.
Before the time I did Lysander see,
Seemed Athens as a paradise to me.
O, then, what graces in my love do dwell
That he hath turned a heaven unto a hell!

LYSANDER

Helen, to you our minds we will unfold.
To-morrow night, when Phoebe doth behold   209
Her silver visage in the wat'ry glass,
Decking with liquid pearl the bladed grass
(A time that lovers' flights doth still conceal),   212
Through Athens gates have we devised to steal.

HERMIA

And in the wood where often you and I
Upon faint primrose beds were wont to lie,   215
Emptying our bosoms of their counsel sweet,
There my Lysander and myself shall meet,
And thence from Athens turn away our eyes
To seek new friends and stranger companies.   219
Farewell, sweet playfellow. Pray thou for us;
And good luck grant thee thy Demetrius.
Keep word, Lysander. We must starve our sight
From lovers' food till morrow deep midnight.

LYSANDER

I will, my Hermia.   *Exit Hermia.*
                    Helena, adieu.
As you on him, Demetrius dote on you.   *Exit Lysander.*

209 *Phoebe* the moon, or Diana 212 *still* always 215 *wont* accustomed
219 *stranger companies* the company of strangers

HELENA

226 How happy some o'er other some can be!
Through Athens I am thought as fair as she.
But what of that? Demetrius thinks not so;
He will not know what all but he do know.
And as he errs, doting on Hermia's eyes,
231 So I, admiring of his qualities.
232 Things base and vile, holding no quantity,
Love can transpose to form and dignity.
Love looks not with the eyes, but with the mind,
And therefore is winged Cupid painted blind.
236 Nor hath Love's mind of any judgment taste;
237 Wings, and no eyes, figure unheedy haste.
And therefore is Love said to be a child,
Because in choice he is so oft beguiled.
240 As waggish boys in game themselves forswear,
So the boy Love is perjured everywhere.
242 For ere Demetrius looked on Hermia's eyne,
He hailed down oaths that he was only mine;
And when this hail some heat from Hermia felt,
So he dissolved, and show'rs of oaths did melt.
I will go tell him of fair Hermia's flight.
Then to the wood will he to-morrow night
248 Pursue her; and for this intelligence
249 If I have thanks, it is a dear expense.
But herein mean I to enrich my pain,
To have his sight thither and back again.   *Exit.*

*

226 *other some* other persons 231 *admiring of* marvelling at; *qualities* gifts, 'parts' 232 *holding no quantity* i.e. without dimension, therefore shapeless, unlovely 236 *Nor . . . taste* (since love resides in the imagination, not in the reason) 237 *figure* symbolize 240 *waggish* playful; *in game* in fun 242 *eyne* eyes (an old plural) 248 *intelligence* piece of news 249 *a dear expense* i.e. an expense very much worth incurring, a trouble worth taking

38

Enter Quince the Carpenter, and Snug the Joiner, I, ii
and Bottom the Weaver, and Flute the Bellows-
mender, and Snout the Tinker, and Starveling the
Tailor.

QUINCE Is all our company here?

BOTTOM You were best to call them generally, man by 2
man, according to the scrip. 3

QUINCE Here is the scroll of every man's name which is
thought fit, through all Athens, to play in our interlude 5
before the Duke and the Duchess on his wedding day at
night.

BOTTOM First, good Peter Quince, say what the play
treats on, then read the names of the actors, and so grow
to a point.

QUINCE Marry, our play is 'The most lamentable 11
comedy and most cruel death of Pyramus and Thisby.'

BOTTOM A very good piece of work, I assure you, and a
merry. Now, good Peter Quince, call forth your actors
by the scroll. Masters, spread yourselves.

QUINCE Answer as I call you. Nick Bottom the weaver.

BOTTOM Ready. Name what part I am for, and proceed.

QUINCE You, Nick Bottom, are set down for Pyramus.

BOTTOM What is Pyramus? a lover, or a tyrant? 19

QUINCE A lover that kills himself, most gallant, for love.

BOTTOM That will ask some tears in the true performing
of it. If I do it, let the audience look to their eyes. I will
move storms; I will condole in some measure. To the 23
rest. Yet my chief humor is for a tyrant. I could play 24

I, ii The house of Quince (?) **s.d.** (J. D. Wilson points out that the craftsmen are all appropriately named: *Quince* probably for 'quoins' or 'quines,'
wedge-shaped pieces of wood used in building; *Snug* for the tightness of
the joints necessary in cabinet-making; *Bottom* for the reel on which
thread is wound; *Flute* perhaps for the fluted church-organs he would
have to mend; *Snout* for the spout of a kettle; *Starveling* for the proverbial
thinness of tailors) **2** *generally* (Bottom intends the reverse, i.e. individually) **3** *scrip* script **5** *interlude* short play, comedy **11** *Marry* (light
interjection; originally an oath by the Virgin Mary) **19** *lover . . . tyrant*
(typical roles in plays of the time) **23** *condole* lament **24** *humor* (1)
temperamental bent, (2) whim

25 Ercles rarely, or a part to tear a cat in, to make all split.
                    'The raging rocks
                    And shivering shocks
                    Shall break the locks
                        Of prison gates,
30   And Phibbus' car   *Apollo*
                    Shall shine from far   *gods and*
                    And make and mar   *love ridiculed*
                        The foolish Fates.'
    This was lofty. Now name the rest of the players. This
35 is Ercles' vein, a tyrant's vein. A lover is more condoling.
    QUINCE Francis Flute the bellows-mender.
    FLUTE Here, Peter Quince.
    QUINCE Flute, you must take Thisby on you.
39 FLUTE What is Thisby? a wand'ring knight?
    QUINCE It is the lady that Pyramus must love.
    FLUTE Nay, faith, let not me play a woman. I have a beard
        coming.
43 QUINCE That's all one. You shall play it in a mask, and
        you may speak as small as you will.
45 BOTTOM   An I may hide my face, let me play Thisby too.
        I'll speak in a monstrous little voice :–'Thisne, Thisne !'
        'Ah, Pyramus, my lover dear, thy Thisby dear, and lady
        dear !'
    QUINCE No, no, you must play Pyramus; and Flute, you
        Thisby.
    BOTTOM Well, proceed.
    QUINCE Robin Starveling the tailor.
    STARVELING Here, Peter Quince.
54 QUINCE Robin Starveling, you must play Thisby's
        mother. Tom Snout the tinker.
    SNOUT Here, Peter Quince.

---

25 *Ercles* Hercules (a stock ranting part; cf. Seneca, *Hercules Furens*); *to tear
... all split* (common expressions for stage ranting)   **30** *Phibbus' car* chariot
of Phoebus Apollo the sun god (the style parodies early translations of
Seneca)   **35** *condoling* sorrowing, pathetic   **39** *wand'ring knight* knight-
errant (another typical role)   **43** *That's all one* it makes no difference
45 *An* if   **54–55** *Thisby's mother* (see note 57 opposite)

QUINCE You, Pyramus' father; myself, Thisby's father; 57
Snug, the joiner, you the lion's part. And I hope here is
a play fitted. 59

SNUG Have you the lion's part written? Pray you, if it be,
give it me, for I am slow of study.

QUINCE You may do it extempore, for it is nothing but
roaring.

BOTTOM Let me play the lion too. I will roar that I will do 64
any man's heart good to hear me. I will roar that I will
make the Duke say, 'Let him roar again; let him roar
again.'

QUINCE An you should do it too terribly, you would 68
fright the Duchess and the ladies, that they would
shriek; and that were enough to hang us all.

ALL That would hang us, every mother's son.

BOTTOM I grant you, friends, if you should fright the
ladies out of their wits, they would have no more discretion but to hang us; but I will aggravate my voice so 74
that I will roar you as gently as any sucking dove; I will 75
roar you an 'twere any nightingale. 76

QUINCE You can play no part but Pyramus; for Pyramus
is a sweet-faced man, a proper man as one shall see in a 78
summer's day, a most lovely gentlemanlike man. Therefore you must needs play Pyramus.

BOTTOM Well, I will undertake it. What beard were I
best to play it in?

QUINCE Why, what you will.

BOTTOM I will discharge it in either your straw-color 84
beard, your orange-tawny beard, your purple-in-grain 85

---

57 *Pyramus' father, Thisby's father* (the parents are mentioned in the source
story, but they do not appear in the interlude as acted) **59** *fitted* cast
64 *that* so that **68** *An* if **74** *aggravate* (Bottom means the opposite, i.e.
diminish, soften) **75** *roar you* (a colloquialism, with vague sense of 'roar for
you') **76** *an 'twere* as if it were **78** *proper* fine, handsome **84–85** *your . . .
beard* i.e. one of those straw-color beards you know about (a colloquial use
of 'your') **85** *orange-tawny* brownish orange or merely orange ('tawny'
from '*tanné*,' tanned); *purple-in-grain* i.e. dyed with a fast purple or red
(from 'grain,' name given the dried cochineal insects)

86 beard, or your French-crown-color beard, your perfit
     yellow.

87 QUINCE Some of your French crowns have no hair at all,
     and then you will play barefaced. But masters, here are

89 your parts; and I am to entreat you, request you, and

90 desire you to con them by to-morrow night; and meet
     me in the palace wood, a mile without the town, by
     moonlight. There will we rehearse; for if we meet in the

93 city, we shall be dogged with company, and our devices

94 known. In the meantime I will draw a bill of properties,
     such as our play wants. I pray you fail me not.

     BOTTOM We will meet, and there we may rehearse most

97 obscenely and courageously. Take pains, be perfit.
     Adieu.

     QUINCE At the Duke's Oak we meet.

99 BOTTOM Enough. Hold, or cut bowstrings.   *Exeunt.*

*

II, i   *Enter a Fairy at one door, and Robin Goodfellow
               [Puck] at another.*

       PUCK
          How now, spirit, whither wander you?
          FAIRY   Over hill, over dale,
3   Thorough bush, thorough brier,
4   Over park, over pale,
5   Thorough flood, thorough fire;
                   I do wander everywhere,
7   Swifter than the moon's sphere;

---

86 *French-crown-color* i.e. color of the gold coin; *perfit* perfect   87 *French
crowns* heads bald from French disease (syphilis)   89 *am to* have to   90 *con*
learn by heart   93 *devices* purposes, plans   94 *bill* list   97 *obscenely* (better
leave the sense to Bottom!)   99 *Hold ... bowstrings* i.e. keep your promise
or be disgraced (probable sense; an archer's expression of uncertain
meaning)
II, i A wood outside Athens   3 *Thorough* (common dissyllabic form of
'through')   4 *pale* enclosure (here, synonymous with *park*)   5 *flood* water
7 *moon's* (sometimes read as dissyllabic, as in the old genitive form 'moones')

42

And I serve the Fairy Queen,
To dew her orbs upon the green. 9
The cowslips tall her pensioners be. 10
In their gold coats spots you see:
Those be rubies, fairy favors;
In those freckles live their savors. 13
I must go seek some dewdrops here,
And hang a pearl in every cowslip's ear.
Farewell, thou lob of spirits; I'll be gone. 16
Our Queen and all her elves come here anon.

PUCK

The King doth keep his revels here to-night.
Take heed the Queen come not within his sight.
For Oberon is passing fell and wrath, 20
Because that she, as her attendant, hath
A lovely boy, stolen from an Indian king;
She never had so sweet a changeling. 23
And jealous Oberon would have the child 24
Knight of his train, to trace the forests wild. 25
But she perforce withholds the lovèd boy, 26
Crowns him with flowers, and makes him all her joy.
And now they never meet in grove or green,
By fountain clear or spangled starlight sheen, 29
But they do square, that all their elves, for fear, 30
Creep into acorn cups and hide them there.

FAIRY

Either I mistake your shape and making quite,
Or else you are that shrewd and knavish sprite 33
Called Robin Goodfellow. Are not you he 34
That frights the maidens of the villagery, 35

---

9 *orbs* circles (here, fairy rings)   10 *pensioners* members of the royal body-guard, in splendid uniforms   13 *savors* scent   16 *lob* lubber, lout   20 *passing fell and wrath* surpassingly fierce and wrathful   23 *changeling* (tri-syllabic)   24 *jealous* envious   25 *trace* range through   26 *perforce* by force   29 *fountain* spring   30 *square* fall out, quarrel   33 *shrewd* naughty (literally, evil, 'cursed,' but generally used in weaker senses)   34 *Robin Goodfellow* (name for the household elf common in country folklore)   35 *villagery* villagers

36   Skim milk, and sometimes labor in the quern,
37   And bootless make the breathless housewife churn,
38   And sometime make the drink to bear no barm,
     Mislead night-wanderers, laughing at their harm?
40   Those that Hobgoblin call you, and sweet Puck,
     You do their work, and they shall have good luck.
     Are not you he?

PUCK   Thou speakest aright;
     I am that merry wanderer of the night.
     I jest to Oberon, and make him smile
     When I a fat and bean-fed horse beguile,
     Neighing in likeness of a filly foal;
47   And sometime lurk I in a gossip's bowl
48   In very likeness of a roasted crab,
     And when she drinks, against her lips I bob
     And on her withered dewlap pour the ale.
51   The wisest aunt, telling the saddest tale,
     Sometime for three-foot stool mistaketh me;
     Then slip I from her bum, down topples she,
54   And 'tailor' cries, and falls into a cough;
55   And then the whole quire hold their hips and laugh,
56   And waxen in their mirth, and neeze, and swear
     A merrier hour was never wasted there.
     But room, fairy: here comes Oberon.

FAIRY
     And here my mistress. Would that he were gone!
        *Enter [Oberon,] the King of Fairies, at one door, with
        his Train; and the Queen [Titania,] at another, with hers.*

OBERON
     Ill met by moonlight, proud Titania.

---

36 *quern* handmill for grinding pepper, malt, etc.   37 *bootless* without
reward (because the butter won't come); *housewife* (pronounced 'huz-if')
38 *barm* head on the ale   40 *Hobgoblin* Robin the goblin ('Hob' is a country
form of Robert or Robin); *Puck* (a generic name, from Anglo-Saxon
'*puca*,' for mischievous devils or imps)   47 *gossip's* old woman's, crony's
48 *crab* crab apple   51 *aunt* old dame; *saddest* most serious   54 *tailor*
(proverbial exclamation, apparently because tailors sit on the floor to sew)
55 *quire* company, 'chorus'   56 *waxen* increase; *neeze* sneeze

TITANIA

What, jealous Oberon? Fairy, skip hence. 61
I have forsworn his bed and company.

OBERON

Tarry, rash wanton. Am not I thy lord? 63

TITANIA

Then I must be thy lady; but I know
When thou hast stolen away from fairyland,
And in the shape of Corin sat all day, 66
Playing on pipes of corn, and versing love 67
To amorous Phillida. Why art thou here, 68
Come from the farthest steep of India,
But that, forsooth, the bouncing Amazon,
Your buskined mistress and your warrior love, 71
To Theseus must be wedded, and you come
To give their bed joy and prosperity?

Oberon brags of conquests

OBERON

How canst thou thus, for shame, Titania,
Glance at my credit with Hippolyta,
Knowing I know thy love to Theseus?
Didst thou not lead him through the glimmering night
From Perigenia, whom he ravishèd? 78
And make him with fair Aegles break his faith, 79
With Ariadne, and Antiopa? 80

TITANIA

These are the forgeries of jealousy;

jealous feud between Titania + Oberon

61 *jealous* envious; *Fairy* i.e. the fairy who has been talking with Robin (most editors follow Theobald's change to 'Fairies') 63 *rash wanton* willful creature ('wanton' means, literally, 'undisciplined') 66, 68 *Corin, Phillida* (typical names for a shepherd and shepherdess in pastoral poetry) 67 *pipes of corn* pipes made of grain stalks, usually oats 71 *buskined* in buskins, a kind of leather legging 78 *Perigenia* (in Plutarch *Perigouna*, one of Theseus' several mistresses) 79 *Aegles* (North's spelling, which Shakespeare evidently followed, for *Aegle*, another of Theseus' mistresses) 80 *Ariadne* daughter of Minos of Crete who helped Theseus thread the labyrinth to kill the Minotaur and was abandoned by him on an island on his return to Athens; *Antiopa* a name given by some historians, instead of *Hippolyta*, to the Amazonian queen conquered by Theseus

82 And never, since the middle summer's spring,
     Met we on hill, in dale, forest, or mead,
84 By pavèd fountain or by rushy brook,
85 Or in the beachèd margent of the sea,
86 To dance our ringlets to the whistling wind,
     But with thy brawls thou hast disturbed our sport.
     Therefore the winds, piping to us in vain,
     As in revenge, have sucked up from the sea
90 Contagious fogs; which falling in the land
91 Hath every pelting river made so proud
92 That they have overborne their continents.
     The ox hath therefore stretched his yoke in vain,
94 The ploughman lost his sweat, and the green corn
     Hath rotted ere his youth attained a beard;
     The fold stands empty in the drownèd field,
97 And crows are fatted with the murrion flock;
98 The nine men's morris is filled up with mud;
99 And the quaint mazes in the wanton green
     For lack of tread are undistinguishable.
101 The human mortals want their winter here;
102 No night is now with hymn or carol blest.
103 Therefore the moon, the governess of floods,
     Pale in her anger, washes all the air,
105 That rheumatic diseases do abound.

Handwritten margin notes: discordant mixture of elements; river – noble + just when within its bounds; corn = fertility; mazes = human wit; natural separation between things are blurred, confusion

---

82 *middle summer's spring* beginning of midsummer   84 *pavèd* i.e. with a pebbly bottom   85 *margent* margin   86 *ringlets* dances in a ring   90 *Contagious* pestilential   91 *pelting* paltry   92 *continents* containing banks 94 *corn* grain of any kind   97 *murrion flock* flock smitten with the murrain, a disease of sheep and cattle   98 *nine men's morris* square cut in the turf for a game played with counters   99 *quaint mazes* intricate 'paths laid out like a maze to be followed rapidly on foot; *wanton* rank   101 *want . . . here* lack winter as well as other seasons (?), would like winter now as more tolerable than the present summer (?) (Most editors adopt Theobald's emendation, 'cheer' for 'here.')   102 *hymn or carol* i.e. of the Christmas season (probably not hymns to the moon)   103–05 *Therefore . . . abound* i.e. not because hymns to the moon are neglected, but because the fairies are quarrelling (cf. ll. 88, 93)   103 *floods* (1) tides, (2) inundations generally 105 *That* so that; *rheumatic diseases* colds and grippe as well as rheumatism (accented here 'rheùmatic')

And thorough this distemperature we see 106
The seasons alter: hoary-headed frosts
Fall in the fresh lap of the crimson rose,
And on old Hiems' thin and icy crown 109
An odorous chaplet of sweet summer buds
Is, as in mockery, set. The spring, the summer,
The childing autumn, angry winter change 112
Their wonted liveries; and the mazèd world, 113
By their increase, now knows not which is which. 114
And this same progeny of evils comes
From our debate, from our dissension; 116
We are their parents and original.

OBERON
Do you amend it then; it lies in you.
Why should Titania cross her Oberon?
I do but beg a little changeling boy
To be my henchman. 121

TITANIA   Set your heart at rest.
The fairyland buys not the child of me. 122
His mother was a vot'ress of my order, 123
And in the spicèd Indian air, by night,
Full often hath she gossiped by my side,
And sat with me on Neptune's yellow sands,
Marking th' embarkèd traders on the flood; 127
When we have laughed to see the sails conceive
And grow big-bellied with the wanton wind; 129
Which she, with pretty and with swimming gait
Following (her womb then rich with my young squire),
Would imitate, and sail upon the land
To fetch me trifles, and return again,
As from a voyage, rich with merchandise.

---

106 *distemperature* disorder in the natural constitution **109** *Hiems'*
winter's **112** *childing* pregnant, fruitful **113** *wonted liveries* accustomed
garments; *mazèd* amazed, bewildered **114** *increase* products **116** *debate*
contention **121** *henchman* page **122** *The fairyland* i.e. the whole of
fairyland **123** *vot'ress* woman who had taken a vow in the order of which
Titania was patroness **127** *traders* trading ships; *flood* flood-tide **129**
wanton sportive, amorous

But she, being mortal, of that boy did die,
And for her sake do I rear up her boy ;
And for her sake I will not part with him.

OBERON

138   How long within this wood intend you stay ?

TITANIA

Perchance till after Theseus' wedding day.
140   If you will patiently dance in our round
And see our moonlight revels, go with us.
142   If not, shun me, and I will spare your haunts.

OBERON

Give me that boy, and I will go with thee.

TITANIA

Not for thy fairy kingdom. Fairies, away !
We shall chide downright if I longer stay.

Exeunt [Titania and her Train].

OBERON

146   Well, go thy way. Thou shalt not from this grove
147   Till I torment thee for this injury.
My gentle Puck, come hither. Thou rememb'rest
149   Since once I sat upon a promontory
150   And heard a mermaid, on a dolphin's back,
151   Uttering such dulcet and harmonious breath
152   That the rude sea grew civil at her song,
And certain stars shot madly from their spheres
To hear the sea-maid's music.

PUCK   I remember.

OBERON

That very time I saw (but thou couldst not)
Flying between the cold moon and the earth
Cupid, all armed. A certain aim he took

---

138 *stay* (a noun, object of *intend*)   **140** *round* round dance (cf. *ringlets*, II, i, 86)   **142** *shun, spare* (synonyms)   **146** *from* go from   **147** *injury* insult   **149** *Since* when   **150** *mermaid* (equivalent to 'siren' in Renaissance dictionaries)   **151** *dulcet* sweet; *breath* voice, song   **152** *civil* mannerly, gentle

At a fair vestal, thronèd by the west,   158
And loosed his love-shaft smartly from his bow,   159
As it should pierce a hundred thousand hearts.   160
But I might see young Cupid's fiery shaft
Quenched in the chaste beams of the wat'ry moon,   162
And the imperial vot'ress passèd on,
In maiden meditation, fancy-free.   164
Yet marked I where the bolt of Cupid fell.
It fell upon a little western flower,
Before milk-white, now purple with love's wound,
And maidens call it love-in-idleness.   168
Fetch me that flow'r; the herb I showed thee once.   satanic,
The juice of it, on sleeping eyelids laid,   mischevous
Will make or man or woman madly dote   but   171
Upon the next live creature that it sees.   harmless
Fetch me this herb, and be thou here again
Ere the Leviathan can swim a league.   174

PUCK
  I'll put a girdle round about the earth
  In forty minutes.   [Exit.]
OBERON   Having once this juice,
  I'll watch Titania when she is asleep
  And drop the liquor of it in her eyes.   178
  The next thing then she, waking, looks upon
  (Be it on lion, bear, or wolf, or bull,
  On meddling monkey, or on busy ape)   181
  She shall pursue it with the soul of love.

---

158 *vestal* virgin priestess (an allusion to Elizabeth, the Virgin Queen; she is fancied as a votaress of Diana, the virgin moon-goddess; cf. ll. 161–64); *by the west* i.e. in England   **159** *love-shaft* i.e. the golden arrow (cf. I, i, 170)   **160** *As* as if   **162** *wat'ry moon* (cf. II, i, 103)   **164** *fancy-free* free of love-thoughts   **168** *love-in-idleness* the pansy (the fanciful metamorphosis in these lines may have been suggested by the change of the mulberries from white to purple by the blood of Pyramus, in Ovid, *Metamorphoses*, IV, 125–27)   **171** *or . . . or* either . . . or   **174** *Leviathan* Biblical sea-monster, usually identified with the whale   **178** *liquor of it* juice of the flower (?), or essence of the juice (?)   **181** *busy* meddlesome (cf. 'busybody')

And ere I take this charm from off her sight
(As I can take it with another herb)
I'll make her render up her page to me.
But who comes here? I am invisible,
And I will overhear their conference.
    Enter Demetrius, Helena following him.

DEMETRIUS

I love thee not; therefore pursue me not.
Where is Lysander and fair Hermia?
The one I'll slay, the other slayeth me.
Thou told'st me they were stol'n unto this wood;
192   And here am I, and wood within this wood
Because I cannot meet my Hermia.
Hence, get thee gone, and follow me no more!

HELENA

195   You draw me, you hard-hearted adamant!
196   But yet you draw not iron, for my heart
Is true as steel. Leave you your power to draw,
And I shall have no power to follow you.

DEMETRIUS

Do I entice you? Do I speak you fair?
Or rather do I not in plainest truth
Tell you I do not nor I cannot love you?

HELENA

And even for that do I love you the more.
I am your spaniel; and Demetrius,
The more you beat me, I will fawn on you.
Use me but as your spaniel – spurn me, strike me,
Neglect me, lose me; only give me leave
(Unworthy as I am) to follow you.
What worser place can I beg in your love
(And yet a place of high respect with me)
Than to be usèd as you use your dog?

---

192 *and wood* and mad   **195** *adamant* (1) loadstone or magnet, (2) the
hardest stone, diamond (often thought to be the same fabulous stone)
196–97 *But . . . steel* i.e. but in drawing me, you are attracting not base iron
but refined steel, which will hold its temper

DEMETRIUS

> Tempt not too much the hatred of my spirit,
> For I am sick when I do look on thee.

HELENA

> And I am sick when I look not on you.

DEMETRIUS

> You do impeach your modesty too much   214
> To leave the city and commit yourself
> Into the hands of one that loves you not,
> To trust the opportunity of night
> And the ill counsel of a desert place   218
> With the rich worth of your virginity.

HELENA

> Your virtue is my privilege. For that   220
> It is not night when I do see your face,
> Therefore I think I am not in the night;
> Nor doth this wood lack worlds of company,
> For you, in my respect, are all the world.   224
> Then how can it be said I am alone
> When all the world is here to look on me?

DEMETRIUS

> I'll run from thee and hide me in the brakes   227
> And leave thee to the mercy of wild beasts.

HELENA

> The wildest hath not such a heart as you.
> Run when you will. The story shall be changed:
> Apollo flies and Daphne holds the chase,   231
> The dove pursues the griffon, the mild hind   232
> Makes speed to catch the tiger – bootless speed,
> When cowardice pursues, and valor flies.

DEMETRIUS

> I will not stay thy questions. Let me go!   235

214 *impeach* call in question, discredit 218 *desert* deserted, wild 220 *Your ... privilege* your power to attract is my warrant, gives me my special right to come (?), or your goodness is my guarantee of immunity from danger (?) 224 *respect* opinion 227 *brakes* thickets 231 *Apollo . . . chase* (Daphne fled from Apollo and was changed into a laurel tree) 232 *griffon* fabulous eagle-headed animal with the body of a lion; *hind* doe 235 *stay* wait for

Or if thou follow me, do not believe
But I shall do thee mischief in the wood.

HELENA

Ay, in the temple, in the town, the field
You do me mischief. Fie, Demetrius.
Your wrongs do set a scandal on my sex.
We cannot fight for love, as men may do;
We should be wooed, and were not made to woo.

[Exit Demetrius.]

I'll follow thee, and make a heaven of hell
To die upon the hand I love so well.   *[Exit.]*

OBERON

Fare thee well, nymph. Ere he do leave this grove,
Thou shalt fly him, and he shall seek thy love.

Enter Puck.

Hast thou the flower there? Welcome, wanderer.

PUCK

Ay, there it is.

OBERON   I pray thee give it me.
I know a bank where the wild thyme blows,

250   Where oxlips and the nodding violet grows,
251   Quite over-canopied with luscious woodbine,
252   With sweet musk-roses, and with eglantine.
253   There sleeps Titania sometime of the night,
       Lulled in these flowers with dances and delight;
       And there the snake throws her enamelled skin,
       Weed wide enough to wrap a fairy in.
       And with the juice of this I'll streak her eyes
258   And make her full of hateful fantasies.
       Take thou some of it and seek through this grove.
       A sweet Athenian lady is in love
       With a disdainful youth. Anoint his eyes;

---

250 *oxlips* species of primrose similar to a cowslip   **251** *over-canopied* (modifies *bank*); *woodbine* honeysuckle (but also applied to different vines; cf. IV, i, 41)   **252** *musk-roses* single, sweet-scented, white garden roses; *eglantine* sweetbrier, a wild rose   **253** *sometime of* at some time during **258** *fantasies* fancies

But do it when the next thing he espies
May be the lady. Thou shalt know the man
By the Athenian garments he hath on.
Effect it with some care, that he may prove
More fond on her than she upon her love ;   266
And look thou meet me ere the first cock crow.

PUCK
Fear not, my lord ; your servant shall do so.   *Exeunt.*

*

Enter Titania, Queen of Fairies, with her Train.   II, ii

TITANIA
Come, now a roundel and a fairy song ;   1
Then, for the third part of a minute, hence –
Some to kill cankers in the musk-rose buds,   3
Some war with reremice for their leathren wings,   4
To make my small elves coats, and some keep back
The clamorous owl, that nightly hoots and wonders
At our quaint spirits. Sing me now asleep.   7
Then to your offices, and let me rest.

Fairies sing.

[1. FAIRY]   You spotted snakes with double tongue,   9
                    Thorny hedgehogs, be not seen ;
              Newts and blindworms, do no wrong,   11
                    Come not near our Fairy Queen.

[Chorus.]

              Philomele, with melody   13
              Sing in our sweet lullaby,
        Lulla, lulla, lullaby ; lulla, lulla, lullaby ;

266 *fond* foolishly doting
II, ii The wood   **1** *roundel* (cf. *ringlets, round*, II, i, 86, 140)   **3** *cankers*
worms, caterpillars; *musk-rose* (cf. II, i, 252)   **4** *reremice* bats   **7** *quaint*
fine, dainty (used of things skillfully made)   **9** *double* forked   **11** *blind-
worms* slow-worms, small snakes   **13** *Philomele* Philomela, the nightingale

Never harm
Nor spell nor charm
Come our lovely lady nigh.
So good night, with lullaby.

1. FAIRY   Weaving spiders, come not here :
Hence, you long-legged spinners, hence !
Beetles black, approach not near ;
Worm nor snail, do no offense.

[Chorus.]

Philomele, with melody, &c.
[She sleeps.]

2. FAIRY   Hence, away ! Now all is well.
One aloof stand sentinel. *[Exeunt Fairies.]*

*Enter Oberon [and squeezes the flower on Titania's
eyelids].*

OBERON   What thou seest when thou dost wake,
Do it for thy true-love take ;
Love and languish for his sake.
Be it ounce or cat or bear,
Pard, or boar with bristled hair
In thy eye that shall appear
When thou wak'st, it is thy dear.
Wake when some vile thing is near. *[Exit.]*

Enter Lysander and Hermia.

LYSANDER
Fair love, you faint with wand'ring in the wood ;
And to speak troth, I have forgot our way.
We'll rest us, Hermia, if you think it good,
And tarry for the comfort of the day.

---

30 *ounce* lynx   **31** *Pard* leopard   **36** *to speak troth* to speak truthfully, 'to
tell the truth'

HERMIA

Be't so, Lysander. Find you out a bed,
For I upon this bank will rest my head.

LYSANDER

One turf shall serve as pillow for us both,
One heart, one bed, two bosoms, and one troth.   42

HERMIA

Nay, good Lysander. For my sake, my dear,
Lie further off yet; do not lie so near.

LYSANDER

O, take the sense, sweet, of my innocence.   45
Love takes the meaning in love's conference.   46
I mean that my heart unto yours is knit,
So that but one heart we can make of it;
Two bosoms interchainèd with an oath –
So then two bosoms and a single troth.   50
Then by your side no bed-room me deny,
For lying so, Hermia, I do not lie.

HERMIA

Lysander riddles very prettily.
Now much beshrew my manners and my pride   54
If Hermia meant to say Lysander lied.
But, gentle friend, for love and courtesy   56
Lie further off, in human modesty.
Such separation as may well be said
Becomes a virtuous bachelor and a maid,
So far be distant; and good night, sweet friend.
Thy love ne'er alter till thy sweet life end.

LYSANDER

Amen, amen, to that fair prayer say I,
And then end life when I end loyalty.
Here is my bed. Sleep give thee all his rest!

42 *troth* true love, pledged faith   45 *take . . . innocence* i.e. take my meaning
in the light of my innocent intentions   46 *Love . . . conference* i.e. when
lovers converse, love interprets the meaning   50 *troth* (cf. l. 42)   54
beshrew curse (common in a very mild sense, as here)   56–57 *gentle
. . . modesty* (an appeal to Lysander as a civilized human being, who is
not a beast or a savage; the implication is in *gentle*, *courtesy*, and *human*)

HERMIA
65   With half that wish the wisher's eyes be pressed!
      [They sleep.]
      Enter Puck.

PUCK   Through the forest have I gone,
              But Athenian found I none
68   On whose eyes I might approve
              This flower's force in stirring love.
              Night and silence! Who is here?
              Weeds of Athens he doth wear.
              This is he (my master said)
              Despisèd the Athenian maid;
              And here the maiden, sleeping sound
              On the dank and dirty ground.
              Pretty soul, she durst not lie
              Near this lack-love, this kill-courtesy.
78   Churl, upon thy eyes I throw
79   All the power this charm doth owe:
              When thou wak'st, let love forbid
              Sleep his seat on thy eyelid.
              So awake when I am gone,
              For I must now to Oberon.   *Exit.*
      Enter Demetrius and Helena, running.

HELENA
      Stay, though thou kill me, sweet Demetrius.
DEMETRIUS
      I charge thee, hence, and do not haunt me thus.
HELENA
86   O, wilt thou darkling leave me? Do not so.
DEMETRIUS
      Stay, on thy peril! I alone will go.   *[Exit.]*
HELENA
88   O, I am out of breath in this fond chase.

---

65 *pressed* closed in sleep   **68** *approve* test, put to the proof   **71** *Weeds*
garments   **78** *Churl* boor, someone without manners (literally, a peasant)
79 *owe* own, possess   **86** *darkling* in the dark   **88** *fond* foolish

The more my prayer, the lesser is my grace.   89
Happy is Hermia, wheresoe'er she lies,
For she hath blessèd and attractive eyes.
How came her eyes so bright? Not with salt tears.
If so, my eyes are oft'ner washed than hers.
No, no! I am as ugly as a bear,
For beasts that meet me run away for fear.
Therefore no marvel though Demetrius
Do, as a monster, fly my presence thus.
What wicked and dissembling glass of mine
Made me compare with Hermia's sphery eyne?   99
But who is here? Lysander, on the ground?
Dead, or asleep? I see no blood, no wound.
Lysander, if you live, good sir, awake.

LYSANDER *[starts up]*
And run through fire I will for thy sweet sake.
Transparent Helena, Nature shows art,   104
That through thy bosom makes me see thy heart.
Where is Demetrius? O, how fit a word
Is that vile name to perish on my sword!

HELENA
Do not say so, Lysander, say not so.
What though he love your Hermia? Lord! what though?
Yet Hermia still loves you. Then be content.

LYSANDER
Content with Hermia? No! I do repent
The tedious minutes I with her have spent.
Not Hermia, but Helena I love.
Who will not change a raven for a dove?
The will of man is by his reason swayed,   115
And reason says you are the worthier maid.
Things growing are not ripe until their season:
So I, being young, till now ripe not to reason.   118

---

89 *grace* answer to prayer, favor   99 *sphery eyne* i.e. eyes as bright as stars in
their spheres   104 *Transparent* (1) ingenuous, able to be seen through, (2)
bright, brilliant   115 *will* desire   118 *ripe not* not ripened

119 And touching now the point of human skill,
     Reason becomes the marshal to my will
121 And leads me to your eyes, where I o'erlook
     Love's stories, written in Love's richest book.

HELENA
     Wherefore was I to this keen mockery born?
     When at your hands did I deserve this scorn?
     Is't not enough, is't not enough, young man,
     That I did never, no, nor never can,
     Deserve a sweet look from Demetrius' eye,
     But you must flout my insufficiency?
129 Good troth, you do me wrong! good sooth, you do,
     In such disdainful manner me to woo.
     But fare you well. Perforce I must confess
132 I thought you lord of more true gentleness.
     O, that a lady, of one man refused,
     Should of another therefore be abused!   *Exit.*

LYSANDER
     She sees not Hermia. Hermia, sleep thou there,
     And never mayst thou come Lysander near.
     For, as a surfeit of the sweetest things
     The deepest loathing to the stomach brings,
     Or as the heresies that men do leave
     Are hated most of those they did deceive,
     So thou, my surfeit and my heresy,
     Of all be hated, but the most of me!
143 And, all my powers, address your love and might
144 To honor Helen and to be her knight.   *Exit.*

HERMIA *[awakes]*
     Help me, Lysander, help me! Do thy best
     To pluck this crawling serpent from my breast.
     Ay me, for pity. What a dream was here!

---

119 *touching . . . skill* i.e. (reason,) now arriving at its maturity   121 *o'erlook*
look over, read   129 *Good troth, good sooth* in truth (merely emphatic
expletives – 'really,' 'indeed,' 'honestly')   132 *gentleness* gentility, good
breeding, courtesy   143 *address* direct, apply   144 *knight* true-love, true
servant

Lysander, look how I do quake with fear.
Methought a serpent eat my heart away,   149
And you sat smiling at his cruel prey.   150
Lysander! What, removed? Lysander! lord!
What, out of hearing? gone? No sound, no word?
Alack, where are you? Speak, an if you hear.   153
Speak, of all loves! I swoon almost with fear.   154
No? Then I well perceive you are not nigh.
Either death, or you, I'll find immediately.   *Exit.*

    Enter the Clowns [Quince, Snug, Bottom, Flute,   III, i
    Snout, and Starveling].

BOTTOM Are we all met?

QUINCE Pat, pat; and here's a marvellous convenient
place for our rehearsal. This green plot shall be our
stage, this hawthorn brake our tiring house, and we will   4
do it in action as we will do it before the Duke.

BOTTOM Peter Quince?

QUINCE What sayest thou, bully Bottom?   7

BOTTOM There are things in this comedy of Pyramus and
Thisby that will never please. First, Pyramus must draw
a sword to kill himself; which the ladies cannot abide.
How answer you that?

SNOUT By'r lakin, a parlous fear.   12

STARVELING I believe we must leave the killing out,
when all is done.

BOTTOM. Not a whit. I have a device to make all well. Write 15
me a prologue, and let the prologue seem to say, we will
do no harm with our swords, and that Pyramus is not
killed indeed; and for the more better assurance, tell

---

149 *eat* ate (pronounced 'et') **150** *prey* act of preying **153** *an if* if **154**
of all loves by all true love
III, i s.d. *Enter the Clowns* (the folio marks an act division here, but the
first quarto indicates that the action was originally continuous, with the
craftsmen rehearsing apart from where Titania lies sleeping) **4** *brake*
thicket or hedge; *tiring house* attiring house, dressing room **7** *bully*
worthy, 'jolly' **12** *By'r lakin* by our Lady; *parlous* 'terrible,' 'awful'
(literally, 'perilous') **15–16** *Write me* i.e. write (a colloquialism, like *roar
you*, I, ii, 75)

them that I Pyramus am not Pyramus, but Bottom the
weaver. This will put them out of fear.

QUINCE Well, we will have such a prologue, and it shall
22   be written in eight and six.

BOTTOM No, make it two more; let it be written in eight
and eight.

SNOUT Will not the ladies be afeard of the lion?

STARVELING I fear it, I promise you.

BOTTOM Masters, you ought to consider with yourselves,
to bring in (God shield us) a lion among ladies is a most
dreadful thing. For there is not a more fearful wild-
fowl than your lion living; and we ought to look to't.

SNOUT Therefore another prologue must tell he is not a
lion.

BOTTOM Nay, you must name his name, and half his face
must be seen through the lion's neck, and he himself
must speak through, saying thus, or to the same defect:
'Ladies,' or 'Fair ladies, – I would wish you' or 'I would
request you' or 'I would entreat you – not to fear, not to
tremble. My life for yours! If you think I come hither as
38   a lion, it were pity of my life. No! I am no such thing.
I am a man as other men are.' And there, indeed, let him
name his name and tell them plainly he is Snug the
joiner.

QUINCE Well, it shall be so. But there is two hard things:
that is, to bring the moonlight into a chamber; for you
know, Pyramus and Thisby meet by moonlight.

SNOUT Doth the moon shine that night we play our play?

BOTTOM A calendar, a calendar! Look in the almanac.
Find out moonshine, find out moonshine.

QUINCE Yes, it doth shine that night.

BOTTOM Why, then may you leave a casement of the
great chamber window, where we play, open, and the
moon may shine in at the casement.

---

22 *eight and six* i.e. lines of eight and six syllables (or four and three stresses)
alternating: the common ballad metre   **38** *it were . . . life* my life would be
in danger

QUINCE Ay. Or else one must come in with a bush of 51
thorns and a lantern, and say he comes to disfigure, or 52
to present, the person of Moonshine. Then there is an- 53
other thing. We must have a wall in the great chamber;
for Pyramus and Thisby, says the story, did talk through
the chink of a wall.

SNOUT You can never bring in a wall. What say you,
Bottom?

BOTTOM Some man or other must present Wall; and let
him have some plaster, or some loam, or some roughcast
about him, to signify wall; and let him hold his fingers
thus; and through that cranny shall Pyramus and
Thisby whisper.

QUINCE If that may be, then all is well. Come, sit down
every mother's son, and rehearse your parts. Pyramus,
you begin. When you have spoken your speech, enter
into that brake; and so every one according to his cue.

Enter Robin [Puck].

PUCK
What hempen homespuns have we swagg'ring here,
So near the cradle of the Fairy Queen?
What, a play toward? I'll be an auditor; 70
An actor too perhaps, if I see cause.

QUINCE Speak, Pyramus. Thisby, stand forth.

PYRAMUS
Thisby, the flowers of odious savors sweet – 73

QUINCE Odorous, odorous.

PYRAMUS ——odors savors sweet;
So hath thy breath, my dearest Thisby dear.
But hark, a voice! Stay thou but here awhile,
And by and by I will to thee appear. *Exit.* 78

51–52 *bush of thorns* bundle of faggots (the man in the moon was traditionally supposed to have a bundle of faggots and a dog; he had been transported to the moon, according to one story, for gathering wood on a Friday) **52** *disfigure* (Quince means 'figure,' i.e. represent) **53** *present* represent (stage term) **70** *toward* on the way **73** *of* (perhaps Pyramus' pronunciation of 'have') **78** *by and by* shortly, presently

PUCK

A stranger Pyramus than e'er played here !   *[Exit.]*

THISBY Must I speak now?

QUINCE Ay, marry, must you. For you must understand he
goes but to see a noise that he heard, and is to come again.

THISBY

Most radiant Pyramus, most lily-white of hue,
 Of color like the red rose on triumphant brier,
85 Most brisky juvenal, and eke most lovely Jew,
 As true as truest horse, that yet would never tire,
 I'll meet thee, Pyramus, at Ninny's tomb.

88 QUINCE 'Ninus' tomb,' man. Why, you must not speak
that yet. That you answer to Pyramus. You speak all
your part at once, cues and all. Pyramus, enter. Your
cue is past; it is 'never tire.'

THISBY

92 O — As true as truest horse, that yet would never tire.
 [Enter Puck, and Pyramus with the ass-head.]

PYRAMUS

93 If I were fair, Thisby, I were only thine.

QUINCE O monstrous! O strange! We are haunted. Pray,
masters! Fly, masters! Help!
 [Exeunt all the Clowns but Bottom.]

PUCK

96 I'll follow you; I'll lead you about a round,
 Through bog, through bush, through brake, through
 brier.
 Sometime a horse I'll be, sometime a hound,
99 A hog, a headless bear, sometime a fire;

---

85 *juvenal* juvenile, youth; *eke* also (archaic in Shakespeare's time); *Jew* (probably added merely to echo *juvenal* and rime with *hue*)   88 *Ninus' tomb* (the lovers' rendezvous in Ovid. Ninus was the mythical founder of Nineveh; his wife Semiramis was supposed to have built the walls of Babylon, the city of Pyramus and Thisbe.)   92 s.d. (no entrance marked in first quarto; folio adds at l. 101 'Enter Piramus with the Asse head.' There was evidently only one ass-head in the property room.)   93 *fair* handsome; *were only* would be only   96 *about a round* roundabout   99 *fire* will-o'- the-wisp

And neigh, and bark, and grunt, and roar, and burn,
Like horse, hound, hog, bear, fire, at every turn. *Exit.*

BOTTOM Why do they run away? This is a knavery of
them to make me afeard.

Enter Snout.

SNOUT O Bottom, thou art changed. What do I see on
thee?

BOTTOM What do you see? You see an ass-head of your
own, do you? *[Exit Snout.]*

Enter Quince.

QUINCE Bless thee, Bottom, bless thee! Thou art trans- 107
lated. *Exit.*

BOTTOM I see their knavery. This is to make an ass of me,
to fright me, if they could. But I will not stir from this
place, do what they can. I will walk up and down here,
and I will sing, that they shall hear I am not afraid. 111

[Sings.]

    The woosel cock so black of hue, 112
      With orange-tawny bill,
    The throstle with his note so true, 114
    The wren with little quill – 115

TITANIA
What angel wakes me from my flow'ry bed?

BOTTOM *[sings]*

    The finch, the sparrow, and the lark,
      The plain-song cuckoo grey, 118
    Whose note full many a man doth mark, 119
      And dares not answer nay.

For, indeed, who would set his wit to so foolish a bird?
Who would give a bird the lie, though he cry 'cuckoo'
never so?

---

107 *translated* transformed 111 *that* so that 112 *woosel* ouzel (English
blackbird or merle, of the thrush family) 114 *throstle* song thrush,
mavis 115 *quill* pipe made of a reed or stalk (by metonymy applied to the
song) 118 *plain-song* i.e. with a song simple and unvarying (as in the
traditional chants of plain-song) 119 *Whose . . . mark* (because in singing
'*cuckoo*' the bird appears to be calling him 'cuckold')

TITANIA

I pray thee, gentle mortal, sing again.
Mine ear is much enamored of thy note;
So is mine eye enthrallèd to thy shape;
127 And thy fair virtue's force (perforce) doth move me,
On the first view, to say, to swear, I love thee.

BOTTOM Methinks, mistress, you should have little
reason for that. And yet, to say the truth, reason and
love keep little company together nowadays. The more
the pity that some honest neighbors will not make them
133 friends. Nay, I can gleek, upon occasion.

TITANIA

Thou art as wise as thou art beautiful.

BOTTOM Not so, neither; but if I had wit enough to get
out of this wood, I have enough to serve mine own
turn.

TITANIA

Out of this wood do not desire to go.
Thou shalt remain here, whether thou wilt or no.
139 I am a spirit of no common rate,
140 The summer still doth tend upon my state;
And I do love thee. Therefore go with me.
I'll give thee fairies to attend on thee,
And they shall fetch thee jewels from the deep,
And sing while thou on pressèd flowers dost sleep;
And I will purge thy mortal grossness so
That thou shalt like an airy spirit go.
147 Peaseblossom, Cobweb, Moth, and Mustardseed!

*Enter four Fairies [Peaseblossom, Cobweb, Moth,
and Mustardseed].*

PEASEBLOSSOM Ready.

---

127 *thy . . . force* the compelling attraction of thy manly charms **133**
gleek make biting jests **139** *rate* rank **140** *still* always, continually;
doth tend upon waits upon, i.e. as one of my train **147** *Moth* i.e. probably
Mote, a speck (both words were usually spelled 'moth,' and both were
pronounced 'mote')

COBWEB
And I.
MOTH   And I.
MUSTARDSEED   And I.
ALL   Where shall we go?
TITANIA
Be kind and courteous to this gentleman.
Hop in his walks and gambol in his eyes;
Feed him with apricocks and dewberries,
With purple grapes, green figs, and mulberries;
The honey-bags steal from the humblebees,   154
And for night tapers crop their waxen thighs,
And light them at the fiery glowworm's eyes,
To have my love to bed and to arise;
And pluck the wings from painted butterflies
To fan the moonbeams from his sleeping eyes.
Nod to him, elves, and do him courtesies.
PEASEBLOSSOM Hail, mortal!
COBWEB Hail!
MOTH Hail!
MUSTARDSEED Hail!
BOTTOM I cry your worships mercy, heartily. I beseech
   your worship's name.
COBWEB Cobweb.
BOTTOM I shall desire you of more acquaintance, good
   Master Cobweb. If I cut my finger, I shall make bold   169
   with you. Your name, honest gentleman?
PEASEBLOSSOM Peaseblossom.
BOTTOM I pray you, commend me to Mistress Squash,   172
   your mother, and to Master Peascod, your father. Good   173
   Master Peaseblossom, I shall desire you of more ac-
   quaintance too. Your name, I beseech you, sir?
MUSTARDSEED Mustardseed.
BOTTOM Good Master Mustardseed, I know your pa-
   tience well. That same cowardly, giantlike ox-beef hath

154 *humblebees* bumblebees **169-70** *If . . . you* (cobweb was used to
stanch blood) **172** *Squash* an unripe pea pod **173** *Peascod* a ripe pea pod

devoured many a gentleman of your house. I promise
you your kindred hath made my eyes water ere now. I
desire you of more acquaintance, good Master Mustardseed.

TITANIA

Come wait upon him; lead him to my bower.
   The moon, methinks, looks with a wat'ry eye;
184   And when she weeps, weeps every little flower,
185   Lamenting some enforcèd chastity.
186   Tie up my lover's tongue, bring him silently.

Exit [Titania with Bottom and Fairies].

*

III, ii   *Enter [Oberon,] King of Fairies.*

OBERON

I wonder if Titania be awaked;
Then, what it was that next came in her eye,
Which she must dote on in extremity.
   [Enter Puck.]
Here comes my messenger. How now, mad spirit?
5   What night-rule now about this haunted grove?

PUCK

My mistress with a monster is in love.
7   Near to her close and consecrated bower,
8   While she was in her dull and sleeping hour,
9   A crew of patches, rude mechanicals,
That work for bread upon Athenian stalls,
Were met together to rehearse a play,
Intended for great Theseus' nuptial day.
13   The shallowest thickskin of that barren sort,
14   Who Pyramus presented in their sport,

184 *she weeps* i.e. causes dew   185 *enforcèd* violated   186 *lover's* (many
editors follow Pope's emendation, 'love's')
III, ii The wood   5 *night-rule* literally, order of conduct in the night – but
perhaps with an overtone of 'misrule'   7 *close* private   8 *dull* drowsy   9
patches (1) 'tatterdemalions' (Dr Johnson), (2) clowns (cf. IV, i, 207);
rude mechanicals unlettered craftsmen   13 *barren sort* stupid company   14
presented acted

Forsook his scene and entered in a brake. 15
When I did him at this advantage take,
An ass's nole I fixèd on his head. 17
Anon his Thisby must be answerèd,
And forth my mimic comes. When they him spy, 19
As wild geese that the creeping fowler eye,
Or russet-pated choughs, many in sort, 21
Rising and cawing at the gun's report,
Sever themselves and madly sweep the sky;
So at his sight away his fellows fly,
And at our stamp here o'er and o'er one falls; 25
He murder cries and help from Athens calls.
Their sense thus weak, lost with their fears thus strong,
Made senseless things begin to do them wrong,
For briers and thorns at their apparel snatch:
Some, sleeves – some, hats; from yielders all things catch.
I led them on in this distracted fear
And left sweet Pyramus translated there, 32
When in that moment (so it came to pass)
Titania waked, and straightway loved an ass.

OBERON
This falls out better than I could devise.
But hast thou yet latched the Athenian's eyes 36
With the love-juice, as I did bid thee do?

PUCK
I took him sleeping (that is finished too)
And the Athenian woman by his side,
That, when he waked, of force she must be eyed. 40
Enter Demetrius and Hermia.

OBERON
Stand close. This is the same Athenian.

15 *scene* stage 17 *nole* noddle, 'noodle' 19 *mimic* burlesque actor or mime
21 *russet-pated choughs* grey-headed jackdaws (russet was homespun cloth,
reddish-brown or grey); *in sort* in a flock 25 *at our stamp* (Robin Goodfellow was known to stamp in a temper, and his stamp was frightening. Most
editors follow Dr Johnson's conjecture, 'at a stump.') 32 *translated*
transformed 36 *latched* moistened, dribbled on (from verb related to
'leak' and 'leach') 40 *That* so that; *of force* necessarily; *eyed* seen, looked at

PUCK

    This is the woman, but not this the man.

DEMETRIUS

    O, why rebuke you him that loves you so?
    Lay breath so bitter on your bitter foe.

HERMIA

    Now I but chide; but I should use thee worse,
    For thou, I fear, hast given me cause to curse.
    If thou hast slain Lysander in his sleep,
    Being o'er shoes in blood, plunge in the deep,
    And kill me too.
    The sun was not so true unto the day
    As he to me. Would he have stolen away
    From sleeping Hermia? I'll believe as soon
53   This whole earth may be bored, and that the moon
    May through the centre creep, and so displease
55   Her brother's noontide with th' Antipodes.
    It cannot be but thou hast murd'red him.
57   So should a murderer look – so dead, so grim.

DEMETRIUS

    So should the murdered look, and so should I,
    Pierced through the heart with your stern cruelty.
    Yet you, the murderer, look as bright, as clear,
61   As yonder Venus in her glimmering sphere.

HERMIA

    What's this to my Lysander? Where is he?
    Ah, good Demetrius, wilt thou give him me?

DEMETRIUS

    I had rather give his carcass to my hounds.

HERMIA

    Out, dog! out, cur! Thou driv'st me past the bounds
    Of maiden's patience. Hast thou slain him then?
    Henceforth be never numb'red among men.

---

53 *whole* intact, i.e. solid   55 *Her brother's* i.e. the sun's; *th' Antipodes* the people on the opposite side of the globe   57 *dead* deadly   61 *sphere* orbit (literally, the hollow sphere in which, according to Ptolemaic astronomy, a planet revolved about the earth)

O, once tell true : tell true, even for my sake.
Durst thou have looked upon him, being awake ?
And hast thou killed him sleeping ? O brave touch !   70
Could not a worm, an adder, do so much ?
An adder did it ; for with doubler tongue
Than thine (thou serpent !) never adder stung.

DEMETRIUS
You spend your passion on a misprised mood.   74
I am not guilty of Lysander's blood,
Nor is he dead, for aught that I can tell.

HERMIA
I pray thee, tell me then that he is well.

DEMETRIUS
An if I could, what should I get therefore ?   78

HERMIA
A privilege never to see me more ;
And from thy hated presence part I so.
See me no more, whether he be dead or no.   *Exit.*

DEMETRIUS
There is no following her in this fierce vein.
Here therefore for a while I will remain.
So sorrow's heaviness doth heavier grow   84
For debt that bankrout sleep doth sorrow owe ;   85
Which now in some slight measure it will pay,
If for his tender here I make some stay.   87
     Lie down [and sleep].

OBERON
What hast thou done ? Thou hast mistaken quite
And laid the love-juice on some true-love's sight.   89
Of thy misprision must perforce ensue   90
Some true-love turned, and not a false turned true.

---

70 *brave touch* noble stroke (ironical)   **74** *misprised mood* mood based on a misunderstanding   **78** *An if* if   **84** *heaviness, heavier* (a quibble on 'heavy' in two senses of 'heavy-spirited' and 'drowsy')   **85** *bankrout* bankrupt **87** *tender* offer; *make some stay* i.e. wait a while; **s.d.** *Lie . . . sleep* (imperative form of stage directions common in Elizabethan plays)   **89** *true-love's* betrothed lover's   **90** *misprision* mistake

PUCK

92   Then fate o'errules, that, one man holding troth,
93   A million fail, confounding oath on oath.

OBERON

About the wood, go swifter than the wind,
And Helena of Athens look thou find.
96   All fancy-sick she is, and pale of cheer
97   With sighs of love, that costs the fresh blood dear.
By some illusion see thou bring her here.
99   I'll charm his eyes against she do appear.

PUCK

I go, I go, look how I go,
Swifter than arrow from the Tartar's bow.   *[Exit.]*

OBERON   Flower of this purple dye,
Hit with Cupid's archery,
Sink in apple of his eye!
When his love he doth espy,
Let her shine as gloriously
As the Venus of the sky.
When thou wak'st, if she be by,
Beg of her for remedy.

Enter Puck.

PUCK   Captain of our fairy band,
Helena is here at hand,
And the youth, mistook by me,
113   Pleading for a lover's fee.
114   Shall we their fond pageant see?
Lord, what fools these mortals be!

OBERON   Stand aside. The noise they make
Will cause Demetrius to awake.

PUCK   Then will two at once woo one:
119   That must needs be sport alone.

---

92 *troth* faith   **93** *confounding* destroying, breaking   **96** *fancy-sick* love-sick; *cheer* face, look   **97** *that . . . dear* (by drawing blood from the heart)   **99** *against . . . appear* in preparation for her appearance   **113** *lover's fee* right as a lover (proverbially three kisses)   **114** *fond pageant* foolish spectacle   **119** *alone* unique, unequalled

> And those things do best please me
> That befall prepost'rously.

Enter Lysander and Helena.

LYSANDER

Why should you think that I should woo in scorn?
  Scorn and derision never come in tears.
Look, when I vow, I weep; and vows so born,
  In their nativity all truth appears.
How can these things in me seem scorn to you,
Bearing the badge of faith to prove them true?   127

HELENA

You do advance your cunning more and more.   128
  When truth kills truth, O devilish-holy fray!   129
These vows are Hermia's. Will you give her o'er?
  Weigh oath with oath, and you will nothing weigh.
Your vows to her and me, put in two scales,
Will even weigh; and both as light as tales.

LYSANDER

I had no judgment when to her I swore.

HELENA

Nor none, in my mind, now you give her o'er.

LYSANDER

Demetrius loves her; and he loves not you.

DEMETRIUS *[awakes]*

O Helen, goddess, nymph, perfect, divine!
To what, my love, shall I compare thine eyne?
Crystal is muddy. O, how ripe in show
Thy lips, those kissing cherries, tempting grow!
That pure congealèd white, high Taurus' snow,   141
Fanned with the eastern wind, turns to a crow   142
When thou hold'st up thy hand. O, let me kiss
This princess of pure white, this seal of bliss.   144

---

127 *badge of faith* (perhaps suggested by family crest worn on sleeves of servants) **128** *advance* put forward so that it can be seen **129** *truth kills truth* i.e. 'truth' to Helena implies falsehood to Hermia **141** *Taurus'* i.e. of the Taurus Mountains in Turkey **142** *Fanned with* (1) blown gently on by, (2) winnowed by **144** *This . . . white* i.e. her hand, 'of sovereign whiteness' (Wilson)

HELENA

O spite! O hell! I see you all are bent
To set against me for your merriment.
147 If you were civil and knew courtesy,
148 You would not do me thus much injury.
Can you not hate me, as I know you do,
But you must join in souls to mock me too?
If you were men, as men you are in show,
152 You would not use a gentle lady so;
153 To vow, and swear, and superpraise my parts,
When I am sure you hate me with your hearts.
You both are rivals, and love Hermia;
And now both rivals to mock Helena.
157 A trim exploit, a manly enterprise,
To conjure tears up in a poor maid's eyes
With your derision! None of noble sort
160 Would so offend a virgin and extort
A poor soul's patience, all to make you sport.

LYSANDER

You are unkind, Demetrius. Be not so!
For you love Hermia: this you know I know.
And here, with all good will, with all my heart,
In Hermia's love I yield you up my part;
And yours of Helena to me bequeath,
Whom I do love, and will do till my death.

HELENA

168 Never did mockers waste more idle breath.

DEMETRIUS

Lysander, keep thy Hermia: I will none.
If e'er I loved her, all that love is gone.
My heart to her but as guestwise sojourned,
And now to Helen is it home returned,
There to remain.

LYSANDER   Helen, it is not so.

---

147 *civil* civilized   148 *injury* insult   152 *gentle* well-born   153 *parts*
qualities   157 *trim* 'fine,' 'nice' (ironical; cf. *brave touch*, III, ii, 70)
160 *extort* wring, twist, torture   168 *idle* vain

DEMETRIUS

Disparage not the faith thou dost not know,
Lest, to thy peril, thou aby it dear.   175
Look where thy love comes. Yonder is thy dear.
      Enter Hermia.

HERMIA

Dark night, that from the eye his function takes,   177
The ear more quick of apprehension makes.
Wherein it doth impair the seeing sense,
It pays the hearing double recompense.
Thou art not by mine eye, Lysander, found;
Mine ear, I thank it, brought me to thy sound.
But why unkindly didst thou leave me so?

LYSANDER

Why should he stay whom love doth press to go?

HERMIA

What love could press Lysander from my side?

LYSANDER

Lysander's love, that would not let him bide –
Fair Helena; who more engilds the night
Than all yon fiery oes and eyes of light.   188
Why seek'st thou me? Could not this make thee know,
The hate I bare thee made me leave thee so?

HERMIA

You speak not as you think. It cannot be.

HELENA

Lo, she is one of this confederacy.
Now I perceive they have conjoined all three
To fashion this false sport in spite of me.   194
Injurious Hermia, most ungrateful maid,   195
Have you conspired, have you with these contrived   196
To bait me with this foul derision?   197

---

175 *aby* pay for   **177** *his* its (the common neuter possessive in Shake-speare's day); *takes* takes away   **188** *oes* round spangles (probably a pun in *oes and eyes*)   **194** *in spite of me* to spite me   **195** *Injurious* insulting   **196** *contrived* plotted, conspired   **197** *bait* torment (literally, to set on dogs to bite, as in bear-baiting)

198   Is all the counsel that we two have shared,
The sister's vows, the hours that we have spent
When we have chid the hasty-footed time
For parting us – O, is all forgot?
All schooldays friendship, childhood innocence?
203   We, Hermia, like two artificial gods,
204   Have with our needles created both one flower,
Both on one sampler, sitting on one cushion,
Both warbling of one song, both in one key;
As if our hands, our sides, voices, and minds
208   Had been incorporate. So we grew together,
Like to a double cherry, seeming parted,
But yet an union in partition –
Two lovely berries moulded on one stem;
So, with two seeming bodies, but one heart;
213   Two of the first, like coats in heraldry,
Due but to one, and crownèd with one crest.
And will you rent our ancient love asunder,
To join with men in scorning your poor friend?
It is not friendly, 'tis not maidenly.
Our sex, as well as I, may chide you for it,
Though I alone do feel the injury.

HERMIA
I am amazèd at your passionate words.
I scorn you not. It seems that you scorn me.

HELENA
Have you not set Lysander, as in scorn,
To follow me and praise my eyes and face?

---

198 *counsel* confidences   203 *artificial* i.e. skillful in artifice or creation
204 *needles* (pronounced 'neelds' or 'neeles'; often so spelled)   208
incorporate in one body   213 *the first* (heraldic term) the first color mentioned in a blazon or description of a shield, or the first quartering described   213–14 *Two . . . crest* (In the shield Helena has in mind, the
coat-of-arms of the bearer evidently appears twice, and the shield is
surmounted by his single crest; in the same way Hermia and Helena have
two bodies, but one heart. Cf. the British royal standard, in which the
three leopards of England appear both in the upper left and in the lower
right quarters.)

And made your other love, Demetrius
(Who even but now did spurn me with his foot),
To call me goddess, nymph, divine, and rare,
Precious, celestial? Wherefore speaks he this
To her he hates? And wherefore doth Lysander
Deny your love (so rich within his soul)
And tender me (forsooth) affection,   230
But by your setting on, by your consent?
What though I be not so in grace as you,   232
So hung upon with love, so fortunate;
But miserable most, to love unloved?
This you should pity rather than despise.

HERMIA
I understand not what you mean by this.

HELENA
Ay, do. Persever, counterfeit sad looks,   237
Make mouths upon me when I turn my back,
Wink each at other, hold the sweet jest up.
This sport, well carried, shall be chronicled.
If you have any pity, grace, or manners,
You would not make me such an argument.   242
But fare ye well. 'Tis partly my own fault,
Which death or absence soon shall remedy.

LYSANDER
Stay, gentle Helena; hear my excuse,
My love, my life, my soul, fair Helena!

HELENA
O excellent!

HERMIA   Sweet, do not scorn her so.

DEMETRIUS
If she cannot entreat, I can compel.

LYSANDER
Thou canst compel no more than she entreat.
Thy threats have no more strength than her weak prayers.
Helen, I love thee; by my life, I do!

230 *tender* offer   232 *grace* favor   237 *Persever* (accented 'persèver')
242 *argument* subject of jest

I swear by that which I will lose for thee
To prove him false that says I love thee not.

DEMETRIUS

I say I love thee more than he can do.

LYSANDER

If thou say so, withdraw and prove it too.

DEMETRIUS

Quick, come!

HERMIA   Lysander, whereto tends all this?

LYSANDER

257 Away, you Ethiope!

DEMETRIUS   No, no, you'll
Seem to break loose, take on as you would follow,
But yet come not. You are a tame man, go!

LYSANDER

Hang off, thou cat, thou burr! Vile thing, let loose,
Or I will shake thee from me like a serpent.

HERMIA

Why are you grown so rude? What change is this,
Sweet love?

263 LYSANDER   Thy love? Out, tawny Tartar, out!
264 Out, loathèd med'cine! O hated potion, hence!

HERMIA

Do you not jest?

265 HELENA   Yes, sooth! and so do you.

LYSANDER

Demetrius, I will keep my word with thee.

DEMETRIUS

I would I had your bond, for I perceive
A weak bond holds you. I'll not trust your word.

LYSANDER

What, should I hurt her, strike her, kill her dead?

257 *No, no, you'll* (the present editor's emendation for 'No, no: heele' of
quartos; folio reads 'No, no, Sir'; many editors follow Lettsom's emendation 'No, no, sir! You')   263 *tawny Tartar* (Hermia's brunette complexion
exaggerated; cf. *Ethiope*, l. 257)   264 *med'cine, potion* (both often used
synonymously with 'poison')   265 *sooth* truly, indeed

Although I hate her, I'll not harm her so.

HERMIA

What, can you do me greater harm than hate?
Hate me? Wherefore? O me, what news, my love?
Am not I Hermia? Are not you Lysander?
I am as fair now as I was erewhile.
Since night you loved me; yet since night you left me.
Why then, you left me (O, the gods forbid!)
In earnest, shall I say?

LYSANDER   Ay, by my life!
And never did desire to see thee more.
Therefore be out of hope, of question, of doubt;
Be certain. Nothing truer. 'Tis no jest
That I do hate thee, and love Helena.

HERMIA

O me! you juggler, you canker blossom,   282
You thief of love! What, have you come by night
And stol'n my love's heart from him?

HELENA   Fine, i' faith.
Have you no modesty, no maiden shame,
No touch of bashfulness? What, will you tear
Impatient answers from my gentle tongue?
Fie, fie, you counterfeit, you puppet you!   288

HERMIA

Puppet? Why, so! Ay, that way goes the game.
Now I perceive that she hath made compare
Between our statures; she hath urged her height,
And with her personage, her tall personage,
Her height (forsooth), she hath prevailed with him.
And are you grown so high in his esteem
Because I am so dwarfish and so low?   295
How low am I, thou painted maypole? Speak!   296

---

282 *canker blossom* wild rose or dog rose (?), or worm that cankers a blossom
(?), or blossom cankered by a worm (?)   **288** *puppet* (1) doll, mere counterfeit of a woman, (2) little person   **295** *low* short   **296** *painted maypole* i.e.
tall, and with pink and white complexion (with a hint that her complexion
isn't all her own?)

How low am I? I am not yet so low
But that my nails can reach unto thine eyes.

HELENA

I pray you, though you mock me, gentlemen,
300 Let her not hurt me. I was never curst;
I have no gift at all in shrewishness;
302 I am a right maid for my cowardice.
Let her not strike me. You perhaps may think,
Because she is something lower than myself,
305 That I can match her.

HERMIA   Lower? Hark again!

HELENA

Good Hermia, do not be so bitter with me.
I evermore did love you, Hermia,
Did ever keep your counsels, never wronged you;
Save that, in love unto Demetrius,
I told him of your stealth unto this wood.
He followed you; for love I followed him.
But he hath chid me hence, and threat'ned me
To strike me, spurn me, nay, to kill me too.
314 And now, so you will let me quiet go,
To Athens will I bear my folly back
And follow you no further. Let me go.
317 You see how simple and how fond I am.

HERMIA

Why, get you gone. Who is't that hinders you?

HELENA

A foolish heart, that I leave here behind.

HERMIA

What, with Lysander?

HELENA   With Demetrius.

LYSANDER

Be not afraid. She shall not harm thee, Helena.

---

300 *curst* shrewish, quarrelsome   **302** *right* downright, real   **305** *match her*
i.e. in a fight   **314** *so* if only   **317** *fond* foolish

DEMETRIUS

    No, sir, she shall not, though you take her part.

HELENA

    O, when she is angry, she is keen and shrewd.   323

    She was a vixen when she went to school;

    And though she be but little, she is fierce.

HERMIA

    'Little' again? nothing but 'low' and 'little'?

    Why will you suffer her to flout me thus?   327

    Let me come to her.

LYSANDER   Get you gone, you dwarf!

    You minimus, of hind'ring knotgrass made!   329

    You bead, you acorn!

DEMETRIUS   You are too officious

    In her behalf that scorns your services.

    Let her alone. Speak not of Helena;

    Take not her part. For if thou dost intend

    Never so little show of love to her,

    Thou shalt aby it.   335

LYSANDER   Now she holds me not.

    Now follow, if thou dar'st, to try whose right,   336

    Of thine or mine, is most in Helena.

DEMETRIUS

    Follow? Nay, I'll go with thee, cheek by jowl.

        [Exeunt Lysander and Demetrius.]

HERMIA

    You, mistress, all this coil is long of you.   339

    Nay, go not back.

HELENA   I will not trust you, I,

    Nor longer stay in your curst company.   341

    Your hands than mine are quicker for a fray;

    My legs are longer, though, to run away.

---

323 *shrewd* shrewish   **327** *flout* mock   **329** *minimus* smallest thing; *knotgrass* a low-growing plant of the buckwheat family that hinders the plough and was thought to stunt the growth of children   **335** *aby* pay for   **336–37** *whose right . . . thine* whose right of the two   **339** *coil* noisy disturbance, 'row'; *long of* because of   **341** *curst* (cf. l. 300)

HERMIA

344   I am amazed, and know not what to say.

Exeunt [Helena and Hermia].

OBERON

This is thy negligence. Still thou mistak'st,
Or else committ'st thy knaveries willfully.

PUCK

Believe me, king of shadows, I mistook.
Did not you tell me I should know the man
By the Athenian garments he had on?
And so far blameless proves my enterprise
That I have 'nointed an Athenian's eyes;

352   And so far am I glad it so did sort
As this their jangling I esteem a sport.

OBERON

Thou seest these lovers seek a place to fight.
Hie therefore, Robin, overcast the night.

356   The starry welkin cover thou anon
357   With drooping fog as black as Acheron,
And lead these testy rivals so astray
As one come not within another's way.
Like to Lysander sometime frame thy tongue,
361   Then stir Demetrius up with bitter wrong;
And sometime rail thou like Demetrius.
And from each other look thou lead them thus
Till o'er their brows death-counterfeiting sleep
365   With leaden legs and batty wings doth creep.
366   Then crush this herb into Lysander's eye,
367   Whose liquor hath this virtuous property,
368   To take from thence all error with his might
369   And make his eyeballs roll with wonted sight.

---

344 *amazed* bewildered, confused   **352** *sort* fall out, happen   **356** *welkin* sky   **357** *Acheron* hell (from the name of one of the rivers of Hades)   **361** *wrong* insults   **365** *batty* bat-like   **366** *this herb* (not *love-in-idleness*, II, i, 166 ff., but another herb; cf. II, i, 184; IV, i, 72)   **367** *liquor* juice; *virtuous* potent, efficacious   **368** *his might* its power   **369** *wonted* accustomed, usual

When they next wake, all this derision 370
Shall seem a dream and fruitless vision, 371
And back to Athens shall the lovers wend
With league whose date till death shall never end. 373
Whiles I in this affair do thee employ, 374
I'll to my queen and beg her Indian boy;
And then I will her charmèd eye release
From monster's view, and all things shall be peace.

PUCK
My fairy lord, this must be done with haste,
For night's swift dragons cut the clouds full fast, 379
And yonder shines Aurora's harbinger; 380
At whose approach ghosts, wand'ring here and there,
Troop home to churchyards; damnèd spirits all, 382
That in crossways and floods have burial,
Already to their wormy beds are gone.
For fear lest day should look their shames upon,
They willfully themselves exile from light,
And must for aye consort with black-browed night. 387

OBERON
But we are spirits of another sort.
I with the Morning's love have oft made sport, 389
And, like a forester, the groves may tread 390
Even till the eastern gate, all fiery red,
Opening on Neptune, with fair blessèd beams
Turns into yellow gold his salt green streams.
But notwithstanding, haste; make no delay.
We may effect this business yet ere day. *[Exit.]*

---

370 *derision* i.e. subject of derision or laughter **371** *fruitless* of no consequence in the world of reality **373** *date* term **374** *Whiles* whilst **379** *night's swift dragons* (probably suggested by Medea's team of dragons, which came down to her following her prayers to Hecate, in Ovid, *Metamorphoses*, VII, 218–21) **380** *Aurora's harbinger* i.e. the morning star **382–83** *damnèd spirits . . . burial* i.e. the ghosts of suicides, who have, according to custom, been buried at crossroads, or who have drowned themselves **387** *for aye* forever **389** *the Morning's love* Cephalus, beloved of Aurora, and a hunter (Ovid, *Metamorphoses*, VII, 700 ff.) **390** *forester* keeper of a royal forest

PUCK   Up and down, up and down,
           I will lead them up and down.
           I am feared in field and town.
399   Goblin, lead them up and down.
        Here comes one.
           Enter Lysander.

LYSANDER
        Where art thou, proud Demetrius? Speak thou now.

PUCK
402   Here, villain, drawn and ready. Where art thou?

LYSANDER
        I will be with thee straight.

PUCK   Follow me then
404   To plainer ground.   *[Exit Lysander.]*
           Enter Demetrius.

DEMETRIUS   Lysander, speak again!
        Thou runaway, thou coward, art thou fled?
        Speak! In some bush? Where dost thou hide thy head?

PUCK
        Thou coward, art thou bragging to the stars,
        Telling the bushes that thou look'st for wars,
409   And wilt not come? Come, recreant! come, thou child!
410   I'll whip thee with a rod. He is defiled
        That draws a sword on thee.

DEMETRIUS   Yea, art thou there?

PUCK
412   Follow my voice. We'll try no manhood here.   *Exeunt.*
           [Enter Lysander.]

LYSANDER
        He goes before me and still dares me on;

---

399 *Goblin* (Puck apparently addresses himself)   402 *drawn* i.e. with sword drawn   404 *plainer* more level and smooth   404, 412 s.d. *Exit Lysander, Enter Lysander* (added in all modern editions to clarify action. But Lysander may have stayed on stage and groped about to suggest the fog; cf. l. 357. The folio has a direction, 'shifting places,' though out of place at l. 416, suggesting a way of managing action with both Lysander and Demetrius on the stage part of the time.)   409 *recreant* coward (literally, one who breaks his faith)   410 *defiled* dishonored   412 see note 404

When I come where he calls, then he is gone.
The villain is much lighter-heeled than I.
I followed fast, but faster he did fly,
That fallen am I in dark uneven way,   417
And here will rest me.
       [Lies down.]   Come, thou gentle day.
For if but once thou show me thy grey light,
I'll find Demetrius and revenge this spite.
     [Sleeps.]
     [Enter] Robin [Puck] and Demetrius.

PUCK

Ho, ho, ho! Coward, why com'st thou not?   421

DEMETRIUS

Abide me, if thou dar'st; for well I wot   422
Thou run'st before me, shifting every place,
And dar'st not stand nor look me in the face.
Where art thou now?

PUCK   Come hither. I am here.

DEMETRIUS

Nay then, thou mock'st me. Thou shalt buy this dear   426
If ever I thy face by daylight see.
Now go thy way. Faintness constraineth me
To measure out my length on this cold bed.
By day's approach look to be visited.
     [Lies down and sleeps.]
     Enter Helena.

HELENA

O weary night, O long and tedious night,
   Abate thy hours. Shine comforts from the east,
That I may back to Athens by daylight
   From these that my poor company detest;
And sleep, that sometimes shuts up sorrow's eye,
Steal me awhile from mine own company.
     Sleep.

---

417 *That* so that   **421** *Ho, ho, ho* (meant as laughter; devil's traditional entrance cry in medieval religious drama)   **422** *Abide* wait for; *wot* know   **426** *buy this dear* pay dearly for this (probably a form of *aby*; cf. III, ii, 175)

PUCK   Yet but three? Come one more.
              Two of both kinds makes up four.
439   Here she comes, curst and sad.
              Cupid is a knavish lad
              Thus to make poor females mad.
          [Enter Hermia.]

HERMIA
    Never so weary, never so in woe,
        Bedabbled with the dew, and torn with briers,
444   I can no further crawl, no further go;
        My legs can keep no pace with my desires.
      Here will I rest me till the break of day.
      Heavens shield Lysander, if they mean a fray!
          [Lies down and sleeps.]

PUCK   On the ground
                  Sleep sound.
                  I'll apply
                  To your eye,
              Gentle lover, remedy.
          [Squeezes the herb on Lysander's eyelids.]
                  When thou wak'st,
                  Thou tak'st
                  True delight
                  In the sight
              Of thy former lady's eye;
              And the country proverb known,
              That every man should take his own,
              In your waking shall be shown:
461   Jack shall have Jill,
                  Naught shall go ill,
463   The man shall have his mare again, and all shall be well.
                                          [Exit.]

---

439 *curst* cross   **444** *go* walk   **461** *Jack, Jill* (common generic names for
'man' and 'woman')   **463** *The man . . . well* (another proverb)   s.d. (The
folio adds the direction, 'They sleepe all the Act,' i.e. either through the
act-interval or through l. 137 of the next act, as divided in the folio. The
first quarto indicates that the action was originally continuous, with the
lovers lying asleep on the stage.)

Enter [Titania,] Queen of Fairies, and [Bottom the]   IV, i
Clown and Fairies [Peaseblossom, Cobweb, Moth,
Mustardseed, and others] ; and the King [Oberon]
behind them.

TITANIA

Come, sit thee down upon this flow'ry bed,
    While I thy amiable cheeks do coy,   2
And stick musk-roses in thy sleek smooth head,   3
    And kiss thy fair large ears, my gentle joy.

BOTTOM Where's Peaseblossom?

PEASEBLOSSOM Ready.

BOTTOM Scratch my head, Peaseblossom. Where's Monsieur Cobweb?

COBWEB Ready.

BOTTOM Monsieur Cobweb, good monsieur, get you your weapons in your hand, and kill me a red-hipped humblebee on the top of a thistle; and, good monsieur, bring me the honey-bag. Do not fret yourself too much in the action, monsieur; and, good monsieur, have a care the honey-bag break not. I would be loath to have you overflowen with a honey-bag, signior. Where's Monsieur Mustardseed?

MUSTARDSEED Ready.

BOTTOM Give me your neaf, Monsieur Mustardseed. 19
Pray you, leave your curtsy, good monsieur. 20

MUSTARDSEED What's your will?

BOTTOM Nothing, good monsieur, but to help Cavalery 22
Cobweb to scratch. I must to the barber's, monsieur; 23
for methinks I am marvellous hairy about the face, and
I am such a tender ass, if my hair do but tickle me, I
must scratch.

IV, i   **2** *amiable* lovable, lovely; *coy* caress   **3** *musk-roses* (cf. II, i, 252)
19 *neaf* fist   **20** *leave your curtsy* i.e. put on your hat (a curtsy was any
customary gesture of respect)   **22** *Cavalery* Cavalier (title of address for
a gallant; Bottom's form suggests the Italian '*cavaliere*')   **23** *Cobweb* (most
editors read *Peaseblossom*, because Cobweb has been sent on an errand;
but the alliteration shows that the slip is probably Shakespeare's)

TITANIA
What, wilt thou hear some music, my sweet love?

BOTTOM I have a reasonable good ear in music. Let's
29   have the tongs and the bones.

TITANIA
Or say, sweet love, what thou desirest to eat.

BOTTOM Truly, a peck of provender. I could munch your
32   good dry oats. Methinks I have a great desire to a bottle
of hay. Good hay, sweet hay, hath no fellow.

TITANIA
I have a venturous fairy that shall seek
35   The squirrel's hoard, and fetch thee new nuts.

BOTTOM I had rather have a handful or two of dried
pease. But I pray you, let none of your people stir me. I
38   have an exposition of sleep come upon me.

TITANIA
Sleep thou, and I will wind thee in my arms.
Fairies, be gone, and be all ways away. *[Exeunt Fairies.]*
41   So doth the woodbine the sweet honeysuckle
Gently entwist; the female ivy so
Enrings the barky fingers of the elm.
O, how I love thee! how I dote on thee!
    [They sleep.]
    Enter Robin Goodfellow [Puck].

OBERON *[advances]*
Welcome, good Robin. Seest thou this sweet sight?
Her dotage now I do begin to pity;
For, meeting her of late behind the wood,
48   Seeking sweet favors for this hateful fool,

29 *tongs and the bones* music made by tongs struck with a key, and by clappers of bone held between the fingers (folio adds direction: 'Musicke Tongs, Rurall Musicke')   **32** *bottle* small bundle   **35** *thee new nuts* (Hanmer read 'thee thence new nuts' to improve the metre, and most editors follow)   **38** *exposition* (Bottom means 'disposition', i.e. inclination)   **41** *woodbine* (applied to various climbing vines; here probably a bindweed or convolvulus)   **41–42** *So . . . entwist* i.e. in this way the morning-glory gently twists round the sweet honeysuckle   **48** *favors* love tokens (here probably flowers)

I did upbraid her and fall out with her.
For she his hairy temples then had rounded
With coronet of fresh and fragrant flowers;
And that same dew which sometime on the buds   52
Was wont to swell like round and orient pearls,   53
Stood now within the pretty flouriets' eyes   54
Like tears that did their own disgrace bewail.
When I had at my pleasure taunted her,
And she in mild terms begged my patience,
I then did ask of her her changeling child;
Which straight she gave me, and her fairy sent
To bear him to my bower in fairyland.
And now I have the boy, I will undo
This hateful imperfection of her eyes.
And, gentle Puck, take this transformèd scalp
From off the head of this Athenian swain;
That, he awaking when the other do,   65
May all to Athens back again repair,   66
And think no more of this night's accidents
But as the fierce vexation of a dream.
But first I will release the Fairy Queen.
        Be as thou wast wont to be;
        See as thou wast wont to see.
        Dian's bud o'er Cupid's flower   72
        Hath such force and blessèd power.
Now, my Titania, wake you, my sweet queen.

TITANIA
My Oberon, what visions have I seen!
Methought I was enamored of an ass.

OBERON
There lies your love.

---

52 *sometime* formerly **53** *Was wont to* used to; *orient pearls* especially
lustrous and precious pearls (from the fact that the best pearls came from
the East) **54** *flouriets'* flowerets' **65** *other* others (common plural) **66**
May they may **72** *Dian's bud* (the herb of II, i, 184 and III, ii, 366 –
perhaps the '*agnus castus*,' said, in old herbals, to preserve chastity);
Cupid's flower (the herb of II, i, 166 – the pansy)

TITANIA   How came these things to pass ?
O, how mine eyes do loathe his visage now !

OBERON
Silence awhile. Robin, take off this head.
Titania, music call, and strike more dead
Than common sleep of all these five the sense.

TITANIA
Music, ho, music ! such as charmeth sleep.

PUCK
Now, when thou wak'st, with thine own fool's eyes peep.

OBERON
Sound, music !
    [Music.]
               Come, my queen, take hands with me.
And rock the ground whereon these sleepers be.
    [Dance.]
Now thou and I are new in amity,

87   And will to-morrow midnight solemnly
88   Dance in Duke Theseus' house triumphantly
And bless it to all fair prosperity.
There shall the pairs of faithful lovers be
Wedded, with Theseus, all in jollity.

     PUCK   Fairy King, attend and mark :
I do hear the morning lark.

94 OBERON   Then, my queen, in silence sad
Trip we after night's shade.
We the globe can compass soon,
Swifter than the wand'ring moon.

     TITANIA   Come, my lord, and in our flight
Tell me how it came this night
That I sleeping here was found
With these mortals on the ground.   *Exeunt.*
Wind horn. Enter Theseus and all his Train [with Hippolyta and Egeus].

---

87 *solemnly* with ceremony (cf. *solemnities*, I, i, 11)   **88** *triumphantly* with festal ceremony (cf. I, i, 19)   **94** *sad* sober

THESEUS

Go, one of you, find out the forester,   102
For now our observation is performed;   103
And since we have the vaward of the day,   104
My love shall hear the music of my hounds.
Uncouple in the western valley; let them go.
Dispatch, I say, and find the forester. *[Exit Attendant.]*
We will, fair Queen, up to the mountain's top
And mark the musical confusion
Of hounds and echo in conjunction.

HIPPOLYTA

I was with Hercules and Cadmus once   111
When in a wood of Crete they bayed the bear   112
With hounds of Sparta. Never did I hear   113
Such gallant chiding; for, besides the groves,
The skies, the fountains, every region near
Seemed all one mutual cry. I never heard
So musical a discord, such sweet thunder.

THESEUS

My hounds are bred out of the Spartan kind:
So flewed, so sanded, and their heads are hung   119
With ears that sweep away the morning dew;
Crook-kneed, and dewlapped like Thessalian bulls;   121
Slow in pursuit, but matched in mouth like bells,   122
Each under each. A cry more tuneable   123

---

102 *forester* manager of the game and the cover in the royal forest (cf. III, ii, 390)   **103** *observation* observance, i.e. of the rite of May (I, i, 167; IV, i, 132)   **104** *vaward . . . day* forepart (literally, vanguard) of the day, morning   **111–13** *I was . . . Sparta* (no corresponding episode in legend about Hippolyta, but in some accounts Theseus was a companion of Hercules in his Amazonian exploits, and hunted the Calydonian boar with other heroes)   **112** *bayed* brought to bay   **113** *hounds of Sparta* (a famous breed in antiquity)   **119** *So* i.e. like the Spartan kind; *flewed* with hanging chaps, or dewlaps; *sanded* of sandy color   **121** *Thessalian* (unexplained: Theseus killed the Marathonian bull, and did perform exploits in Thessaly)   **122–23** *matched . . . each* i.e. with each voice of a different but harmonious pitch, like a chime of bells (a melodious pack was supposed to have in it 'bass,' 'countertenor,' and 'mean' voices)   **123** *cry* noise of the pack, hence the pack itself; *tuneable* in tune, musical

> Was never holloed to nor cheered with horn
> In Crete, in Sparta, nor in Thessaly.
126 Judge when you hear. But soft! What nymphs are these?

EGEUS

> My lord, this is my daughter here asleep;
> And this, Lysander; this Demetrius is;
> This Helena, old Nedar's Helena.
> I wonder of their being here together.

THESEUS

> No doubt they rose up early to observe
> The rite of May; and, hearing our intent,
133 Came here in grace of our solemnity.
> But speak, Egeus. Is not this the day
> That Hermia should give answer of her choice?

EGEUS

> It is, my lord.

THESEUS

> Go, bid the huntsmen wake them with their horns.

> *[Exit an Attendant.]*
> *Shout within. Wind horns. They all start up.*

138 Good morrow, friends. Saint Valentine is past.
> Begin these woodbirds but to couple now?

LYSANDER

> Pardon my lord.
> *[They kneel.]*

THESEUS   I pray you all, stand up.
> I know you two are rival enemies.
> How comes this gentle concord in the world
143 That hatred is so far from jealousy
> To sleep by hate and fear no enmity?

LYSANDER

145 My lord, I shall reply amazedly,
> Half sleep, half waking; but as yet, I swear,
> I cannot truly say how I came here.

---

126 *soft* wait   **133** *our solemnity* i.e. our observance of May Day   **138–39**
Saint Valentine . . . now (according to an old saying, birds begin to mate on
Saint Valentine's Day)   **143** *jealousy* suspicion   **145** *amazedly* confusedly

But, as I think (for truly would I speak),
And now I do bethink me, so it is –
I came with Hermia hither. Our intent
Was to be gone from Athens, where we might,   151
Without the peril of the Athenian law –   152

EGEUS

Enough, enough, my lord! you have enough.
I beg the law, the law, upon his head.
They would have stol'n away; they would, Demetrius,
Thereby to have defeated you and me –   156
You of your wife, and me of my consent,
Of my consent that she should be your wife.

DEMETRIUS

My lord, fair Helen told me of their stealth,
Of this their purpose hither, to this wood,
And I in fury hither followed them,
Fair Helena in fancy following me.   162
But, my good lord, I wot not by what power
(But by some power it is) my love to Hermia,
Melted as the snow, seems to me now
As the remembrance of an idle gaud   166
Which in my childhood I did dote upon;
And all the faith, the virtue of my heart,   168
The object and the pleasure of mine eye,
Is only Helena. To her, my lord,
Was I betrothed ere I saw Hermia,
But, like a sickness, did I loathe this food;   172
But, as in health, come to my natural taste,
Now I do wish it, love it, long for it,
And will for evermore be true to it.

THESEUS

Fair lovers, you are fortunately met.
Of this discourse we more will hear anon.
Egeus, I will overbear your will,

151 *where* wherever   152 *Without* beyond   156 *defeated* (1) cheated, (2)
deprived   162 *in fancy* in love   166 *idle gaud* worthless trinket   168
virtue power   172 *like a sickness* i.e. as in sickness

179 For in the temple, by and by, with us,
These couples shall eternally be knit;
181 And, for the morning now is something worn,
Our purposed hunting shall be set aside.
Away, with us to Athens! Three and three,
We'll hold a feast in great solemnity.
Come, Hippolyta.

[Exeunt Theseus, Hippolyta, Egeus, and Lords.]

DEMETRIUS
These things seem small and undistinguishable,
Like far-off mountains turnèd into clouds.

HERMIA
188 Methinks I see these things with parted eye,
When everything seems double.

HELENA   So methinks;
190 And I have found Demetrius like a jewel,
Mine own, and not mine own.

DEMETRIUS   Are you sure
That we are awake? It seems to me
That yet we sleep, we dream. Do not you think
The Duke was here, and bid us follow him?

HERMIA
Yea, and my father.

HELENA   And Hippolyta.

LYSANDER
And he did bid us follow to the temple.

DEMETRIUS
Why then, we are awake. Let's follow him,
And by the way let us recount our dreams.   *[Exeunt.]*

BOTTOM *[wakes]* When my cue comes, call me, and I will
answer. My next is 'Most fair Pyramus.' Hey-ho. Peter
Quince? Flute the bellows-mender? Snout the tinker?
202 Starveling? God's my life! Stol'n hence, and left me

179 *by and by* shortly   181 *for* because   188 *with parted eye* i.e. with the
two eyes not in focus   190–91 *And I . . . own* i.e. like a jewel found by
accident, and therefore not certainly mine   202 *God's my life* (a common
oath, perhaps contracted from 'God save my life')

92

asleep? I have had a most rare vision. I have had a dream,
past the wit of man to say what dream it was. Man is but
an ass if he go about to expound this dream. Methought
I was – there is no man can tell what. Methought I was,
and methought I had – But man is but a patched fool if   207
he will offer to say what methought I had. The eye of
man hath not heard, the ear of man hath not seen, man's
hand is not able to taste, his tongue to conceive, nor his
heart to report what my dream was. I will get Peter
Quince to write a ballet of this dream. It shall be called   212
'Bottom's Dream,' because it hath no bottom; and I
will sing it in the latter end of our play, before the Duke.
Peradventure, to make it the more gracious, I shall sing
it at her death.   [Exit.]   216

*

Enter Quince, Flute [, Snout, and Starveling].   IV, ii
QUINCE Have you sent to Bottom's house? Is he come
   home yet?
STARVELING He cannot be heard of. Out of doubt he is
   transported.   4
FLUTE If he come not, then the play is marred; it goes not
   forward, doth it?
QUINCE It is not possible. You have not a man in all
   Athens able to discharge Pyramus but he.
FLUTE No, he hath simply the best wit of any handicraft   9
   man in Athens.
QUINCE Yea, and the best person too, and he is a very
   paramour for a sweet voice.
FLUTE You must say 'paragon.' A paramour is (God bless
   us!) a thing of naught.   14

---

207 *a patched fool* i.e. a fool in a motley or particolored suit   212 *ballet* ballad
216 *her death* (probably Thisby's)
IV, ii The house of Quince (?)   4 *transported* (1) carried away by spirits,
(2) 'translated' (cf. III, i, 107)   9 *wit* intellect, 'brain'   14 *a thing of
naught* (1) a wicked thing, (2) a thing of nothing, nought

Enter Snug the Joiner.

SNUG Masters, the Duke is coming from the temple, and
there is two or three lords and ladies more married. If
our sport had gone forward, we had all been made
men.

18 FLUTE O sweet bully Bottom! Thus hath he lost sixpence
a day during his life. He could not have scaped sixpence
20   a day. An the Duke had not given him sixpence a day
for playing Pyramus, I'll be hanged! He would have
deserved it. Sixpence a day in Pyramus, or nothing!

Enter Bottom.

23 BOTTOM Where are these lads? Where are these hearts?

24 QUINCE Bottom! O most courageous day! O most happy
hour!

26 BOTTOM Masters, I am to discourse wonders; but ask me
not what. For if I tell you, I am not true Athenian. I
will tell you everything, right as it fell out.

QUINCE Let us hear, sweet Bottom.

30 BOTTOM Not a word of me. All that I will tell you is, that
the Duke hath dined. Get your apparel together, good
32   strings to your beards, new ribbands to your pumps;
33   meet presently at the palace; every man look o'er his
34   part; for the short and the long is, our play is preferred.
In any case, let Thisby have clean linen; and let not him
that plays the lion pare his nails, for they shall hang out
for the lion's claws. And, most dear actors, eat no onions
nor garlic, for we are to utter sweet breath; and I do not
doubt but to hear them say it is a sweet comedy. No
more words. Away, go, away!   *[Exeunt.]*

❋

18 *bully* (cf. III, i, 7) 18–19 *sixpence a day* i.e. a pension from the Duke of
this much 20 *An* if 23 *hearts* good fellows 24 *courageous* brave, fine (?),
or encouraging, auspicious (?); *happy* lucky, fortunate 26 *am to* have to
30 *word of* word out of 32 *ribbands* (common spelling of 'ribbons') 33
presently right away 34 *preferred* put forward, recommended

Enter Theseus, Hippolyta, and Philostrate [with   V, i
Lords and Attendants].

HIPPOLYTA

'Tis strange, my Theseus, that these lovers speak of.   1

THESEUS

More strange than true. I never may believe
These antic fables nor these fairy toys.   *he is*   3
Lovers and madmen have such seething brains,   *a*
Such shaping fantasies, that apprehend   *rationalist*
More than cool reason ever comprehends.
The lunatic, the lover, and the poet
Are of imagination all compact.   8
One sees more devils than vast hell can hold: *shakespeare*
That is the madman. The lover, all as frantic,   *is a*
Sees Helen's beauty in a brow of Egypt.   *rationalist*
                                              and a   11   *poet*
The poet's eye, in a fine frenzy rolling,
Doth glance from heaven to earth, from earth to heaven;
And as imagination bodies forth
The forms of things unknown, the poet's pen   *poets,*
Turns them to shapes, and gives to airy nothing   *lunatics,*
A local habitation and a name.   *+ lovers*
Such tricks hath strong imagination   *all imagine*
That, if it would but apprehend some joy,   *things and*
It comprehends some bringer of that joy;   *are irrational*   20
Or in the night, imagining some fear,   *the rationalist*
How easy is a bush supposed a bear!   *knows it is a bush*

HIPPOLYTA

But all the story of the night told over,
And all their minds transfigured so together,   *transformation*   24
More witnesseth than fancy's images   *of lovers*
And grows to something of great constancy;   *implies*   26
                                              some
                                              greater

V, i The palace of the Duke   1 *that* that which, what   3 *antic* (1) gro-   *order*
tesque, bizarre, (2) ancient, 'antique'; *fairy toys* i.e. silly tales about   *which*
fairies ('toys' are 'trifles')   5 *fantasies* imaginations   8 *compact* com-   *reason*
posed   11 *brow of Egypt* face of a gypsy, hence dark   20 *comprehends*   *can't*
. . . *joy* i.e. includes as well the imaginary cause of the joy   24 *transfigured*
so together so changed at the same time   26 *constancy* certainty (because
the evidence is uniform or consistent and holds firm)
                                              apprehend,
                                              necessary to
                                              be a little crazy

27   But howsoever, strange and admirable.
      Enter Lovers : Lysander, Demetrius, Hermia, and
      Helena.

THESEUS

Here come the lovers, full of joy and mirth.
Joy, gentle friends, joy and fresh days of love
Accompany your hearts !

LYSANDER   More than to us
Wait in your royal walks, your board, your bed !

THESEUS

32   Come now, what masques, what dances shall we have,
To wear away this long age of three hours
34   Between our after-supper and bedtime ?
35   Where is our usual manager of mirth ?
What revels are in hand ? Is there no play
To ease the anguish of a torturing hour ?
38   Call Philostrate.

PHILOSTRATE   Here, mighty Theseus.

THESEUS

39   Say, what abridgment have you for this evening ?
What masque ? what music ? How shall we beguile
The lazy time, if not with some delight ?

PHILOSTRATE

42   There is a brief how many sports are ripe.
Make choice of which your Highness will see first.
      [Gives a paper.]

THESEUS

44   'The battle with the Centaurs, to be sung

---

27 *howsoever* in any case; *admirable* wonderful **32** *masques* courtly shows
featuring a dance of masked figures **34** *after-supper* last course, dessert
(?), or light evening repast (?) **35** *mirth* entertainment **38** *Philostrate*
(who acts as Master of the Revels; his part in this act is assigned in the
folio to Egeus) **39** *abridgment* pastime, i.e. something to abridge or
shorten the time **42** *brief* list, memorandum **44** *The battle . . . Centaurs*
probably the famous battle following the attempt of the Centaurs to carry
off the bride of Perithous, Theseus' friend (Shakespeare followed the
medieval and Renaissance versions of the legend in making Hercules
present at the battle)

By an Athenian eunuch to the harp.'
We'll none of that. That have I told my love
In glory of my kinsman Hercules.
'The riot of the tipsy Bacchanals,   48
Tearing the Thracian singer in their rage.'
That is an old device, and it was played   50
When I from Thebes came last a conqueror.
'The thrice three Muses mourning for the death   52
Of Learning, late deceased in beggary.'
That is some satire keen and critical,
Not sorting with a nuptial ceremony.   55
'A tedious brief scene of young Pyramus
And his love Thisby; very tragical mirth.'
Merry and tragical? tedious and brief?
That is hot ice and wondrous strange snow.   59
How shall we find the concord of this discord?

PHILOSTRATE
A play there is, my lord, some ten words long,
Which is as brief as I have known a play;
But by ten words, my lord, it is too long,
Which makes it tedious. For in all the play
There is not one word apt, one player fitted.
And tragical, my noble lord, it is,
For Pyramus therein doth kill himself.
Which when I saw rehearsed, I must confess,
Made mine eyes water; but more merry tears
The passion of loud laughter never shed.   70

THESEUS
What are they that do play it?

48–49 *The riot . . . rage* the tearing apart of Orpheus by the Bacchantes
(Ovid, XI, 1 ff.)   **50** *device* show   **52–53** *The thrice . . . beggary* (perhaps
suggested by the title of Spenser's poem, *The Teares of the Muses*, 1591;
complaints of the neglect of learning and poetry were fashionable)   **55**
sorting with befitting   **59** *strange* (probably an error, since an oxymoron
like *hot ice* is wanted; suggested emendations; scorching, scalding, seething, flaming, fiery, sable, sooty, swarthy)   **70** *passion . . . laughter* (usually
explained as 'passionate outburst,' but probably ironic, i.e. the 'grief' of
loud laughter, in keeping with *tragical mirth*)

PHILOSTRATE
Hard-handed men that work in Athens here,
Which never labored in their minds till now;
74 And now have toiled their unbreathed memories
75 With this same play, against your nuptial.

THESEUS
And we will hear it.

PHILOSTRATE   No, my noble lord,
It is not for you. I have heard it over,
And it is nothing, nothing in the world;
79 Unless you can find sport in their intents,
Extremely stretched and conned with cruel pain,
To do you service.

THESEUS   I will hear that play,
For never anything can be amiss
When simpleness and duty tender it.
Go bring them in; and take your places, ladies.

                              [Exit Philostrate.]

HIPPOLYTA
85 I love not to see wretchedness o'ercharged,
And duty in his service perishing.

THESEUS
Why, gentle sweet, you shall see no such thing.

HIPPOLYTA
88 He says they can do nothing in this kind.

THESEUS
The kinder we, to give them thanks for nothing.
Our sport shall be to take what they mistake;
91 And what poor duty cannot do, noble respect
92 Takes it in might, not merit.
93 Where I have come, great clerks have purposèd

74 *unbreathed* unexercised   75 *against* in preparation for   79 *intents* (two
different senses are required by the two participles in l. 80: both 'endeavors,'
which are *stretched* or strained, and 'object of the endeavors,' i.e. the play,
which has to be *conned* or learned)   85 *o'ercharged* overburdened   88 *this
kind* this type of thing   91 *noble respect* generous consideration   92 *Takes
. . . merit* i.e. takes the will for the deed   93 *clerks* scholars

To greet me with premeditated welcomes;
Where I have seen them shiver and look pale,
Make periods in the midst of sentences,
Throttle their practised accent in their fears,   97
And, in conclusion, dumbly have broke off,
Not paying me a welcome. Trust me, sweet,
Out of this silence yet I picked a welcome,
And in the modesty of fearful duty
I read as much as from the rattling tongue
Of saucy and audacious eloquence.
Love, therefore, and tongue-tied simplicity   104
In least speak most, to my capacity.   105
    [Enter Philostrate.]

PHILOSTRATE
So please your Grace the Prologue is addressed.   106

THESEUS
Let him approach.   107
    [Flourish trumpets.] Enter the Prologue [Quince].

PROLOGUE
If we offend, it is with our good will.   108
   That you should think, we come not to offend,
But with good will. To show our simple skill,
   That is the true beginning of our end.
Consider then, we come but in despite.
   We do not come, as minding to content you,
Our true intent is. All for your delight,
   We are not here. That you should here repent you,
The actors are at hand : and, by their show,
You shall know all, that you are like to know.

THESEUS This fellow doth not stand upon points.   118

---

97 *practised accent* rehearsed utterance or speech   **104** *simplicity* artless-
ness, sincerity   **105** *In least* i.e. in speaking least; *to my capacity* according
to my understanding   **106** *addressed* ready   **107** s.d. (folio adds direction
'Flor. Trum.' and notes that Quince speaks the prologue)   **108–17** (the
mispunctuation in the prologue was a common form of humorous trick)
118 *stand upon points* (1) pay attention to marks of punctuation, (2) bother
about niceties

119 LYSANDER He hath rid his prologue like a rough colt; he
120   knows not the stop. A good moral, my lord: it is not
    enough to speak, but to speak true.

   HIPPOLYTA Indeed he hath played on this prologue like a
123   child on a recorder – a sound, but not in government.

   THESEUS His speech was like a tangled chain; nothing
    impaired, but all disordered. Who is next?

    Enter Pyramus and Thisby, and Wall and Moonshine
    and Lion.

PROLOGUE

   Gentles, perchance you wonder at this show;
    But wonder on, till truth make all things plain.
   This man is Pyramus, if you would know;
    This beauteous lady Thisby is certain.
   This man, with lime and roughcast, doth present
    Wall, that vile Wall which did these lovers sunder;
   And through Wall's chink, poor souls, they are content
    To whisper. At the which let no man wonder.
134 This man, with lantern, dog, and bush of thorn,
    Presenteth Moonshine. For, if you will know,
   By moonshine did these lovers think no scorn
    To meet at Ninus' tomb, there, there to woo.
138 This grisly beast (which Lion hight by name)
    The trusty Thisby, coming first by night,
   Did scare away, or rather did affright;
141 And as she fled, her mantle she did fall,
    Which Lion vile with bloody mouth did stain.
143 Anon comes Pyramus, sweet youth and tall,
    And finds his trusty Thisby's mantle slain;
   Whereat, with blade, with bloody blameful blade,
    He bravely broached his boiling bloody breast.
   And Thisby, tarrying in mulberry shade,

---

119 *rough* unbroken   120 *stop* (1) sudden check in a horse's career, (2)
punctuation mark   123 *recorder* wind instrument similar to a flute; *in
government* controlled with skill   134–35 *This man . . . Moonshine* (cf. III, i,
51–52)   138 *hight* is named (archaic in Shakespeare's day)   141 *fall* let
fall   143 *tall* valiant

His dagger drew, and died. For all the rest,
Let Lion, Moonshine, Wall, and lovers twain
At large discourse while here they do remain.   150

THESEUS I wonder if the lion be to speak.   151

DEMETRIUS No wonder, my lord. One lion may, when
many asses do.   *Exit [Prologue, with Pyramus,] Lion,*
                                    Thisby, and Moonshine.

WALL
In this same interlude it doth befall
That I, one Snout by name, present a wall;   154
And such a wall, as I would have you think,
That had in it a crannied hole or chink,
Through which the lovers, Pyramus and Thisby,
Did whisper often, very secretly.
This loam, this roughcast, and this stone doth show
That I am that same wall : the truth is so.
And this the cranny is, right and sinister,   162
Through which the fearful lovers are to whisper.

THESEUS Would you desire lime and hair to speak better ?

DEMETRIUS It is the wittiest partition that ever I heard   165
discourse, my lord.
        [Enter Pyramus.]

THESEUS Pyramus draws near the wall. Silence !

PYRAMUS
O grim-looked night, O night with hue so black,
    O night, which ever art when day is not !
O night, O night, alack, alack, alack,
    I fear my Thisby's promise is forgot.
And thou, O wall, O sweet, O lovely wall,
    That stand'st between her father's ground and mine,
Thou wall, O wall, O sweet and lovely wall,
    Show me thy chink, to blink through with mine eyne.
        [Wall holds up his fingers.]

150 *At large* at length   151 *be to* is going to   154 *interlude* (cf. I, ii, 5)
162 *right and sinister* i.e. running right and left, horizontal   165 *wittiest*
cleverest, most intelligent; *partition* (1) wall, (2) section of an oration

Thanks, courteous wall. Jove shield thee well for this.
But what see I? No Thisby do I see.
O wicked wall, through whom I see no bliss,
Cursed be thy stones for thus deceiving me!

180 THESEUS The wall, methinks, being sensible, should
curse again.

PYRAMUS No, in truth, sir, he should not. 'Deceiving me'
is Thisby's cue. She is to enter now, and I am to spy her
through the wall. You shall see it will fall pat as I told
you. Yonder she comes.

Enter Thisby.

THISBY

O Wall, full often hast thou heard my moans
For parting my fair Pyramus and me.
My cherry lips have often kissed thy stones,
Thy stones with lime and hair knit up in thee.

PYRAMUS

I see a voice. Now will I to the chink,
191   To spy an I can hear my Thisby's face.
Thisby!

THISBY My love! thou art my love, I think.

PYRAMUS

193   Think what thou wilt, I am thy lover's grace;
194   And, like Limander, am I trusty still.

THISBY

And I, like Helen, till the Fates me kill.

PYRAMUS

196   Not Shafalus to Procrus was so true.

THISBY

As Shafalus to Procrus, I to you.

180 *sensible* capable of sensation and perception 191 *an* if 193 *thy lover's grace* i.e. thy gracious lover 194-95 *Limander . . . Helen* (the 'author' of the interlude probably confused two pairs of famous lovers – Leander and Hero, Alexander [Paris] and Helen) 196 *Shafalus . . . Procrus* Cephalus and Procris, another pair of tragic lovers

PYRAMUS

O, kiss me through the hole of this vile wall!

THISBY

I kiss the wall's hole, not your lips at all.

PYRAMUS

Wilt thou at Ninny's tomb meet me straightway?

THISBY

Tide life, tide death, I come without delay.   201

[Exeunt Pyramus and Thisby.]

WALL

Thus have I, Wall, my part dischargèd so;

And, being done, thus Wall away doth go.   *[Exit.]*

THESEUS Now is the mural down between the two 204
neighbors.

DEMETRIUS No remedy, my lord, when walls are so
willful to hear without warning.   207

HIPPOLYTA This is the silliest stuff that ever I heard.

THESEUS The best in this kind are but shadows; and the 209
worst are no worse, if imagination amend them.

HIPPOLYTA It must be your imagination then, and not
theirs.

THESEUS If we imagine no worse of them than they of
themselves, they may pass for excellent men. Here
come two noble beasts in, a man and a lion.

Enter Lion and Moonshine.

LION

You, ladies, you, whose gentle hearts do fear   216

The smallest monstrous mouse that creeps on floor,

May now perchance both quake and tremble here,

When lion rough in wildest rage doth roar.

---

201 *Tide . . . death* come (betide) life, come death   **204** *mural down* wall
down (Pope's famous conjecture; quartos read 'Moon vsed', folio 'morall
downe'; other emendations: 'mure all down,' 'wall down,' 'moon to see')
207 *to hear* as to hear; *without warning* so unexpectedly (?), or without
warning the parents (?)   **209** *in this kind* of this sort, i.e. players   **216**
gentle ladylike

220 Then know that I as Snug the joiner am
221 A lion fell, nor else no lion's dam;
    For if I should as lion come in strife
223 Into this place, 'twere pity on my life.
224 THESEUS A very gentle beast, and of a good conscience.
225 DEMETRIUS The very best at a beast, my lord, that e'er I
    saw.
227 LYSANDER This lion is a very fox for his valor.
    THESEUS True; and a goose for his discretion.
    DEMETRIUS Not so, my lord; for his valor cannot carry
    his discretion, and the fox carries the goose.
    THESEUS His discretion, I am sure, cannot carry his
    valor; for the goose carries not the fox. It is well. Leave
    it to his discretion, and let us listen to the moon.
    MOON
234 This lanthorn doth the hornèd moon present –
235 DEMETRIUS He should have worn the horns on his head.
    THESEUS He is no crescent, and his horns are invisible
    within the circumference.
    MOON
    This lanthorn doth the hornèd moon present.
    Myself the man i' th' moon do seem to be.
    THESEUS This is the greatest error of all the rest. The
    man should be put into the lanthorn. How is it else the
    man i' th' moon?
243 DEMETRIUS He dares not come there, for the candle; for
244 you see it is already in snuff.

220–21 *I . . . dam* i.e. only as Snug the joiner am I either a fierce lion or a
lioness (folio reads: 'I one Snug . . . am, A lion . . . dam,' and most editors
follow, or emend differently) 221 *lion fell* (probably a quibble on two
senses, 'fierce lion' and 'lion's skin') 223 *'twere . . . life* (cf. III, i, 38)
224 *gentle* well-bred, courteous 225 *best at a beast* (a quibble based on
similar pronunciation) 227 *This lion . . . valor* i.e. 'the better part of valor
is discretion' 234 *lanthorn* (pronounced 'lant-horn' or 'lantern'; spelling
probably due to folk etymology, because lanterns were made of horn; note
pun on *hornèd moon*) 235 *on his head* (as a cuckold) 243 *for the candle* for
fear of the candle 244 *in snuff* (1) in need of snuffing, (2) in a passion

HIPPOLYTA I am aweary of this moon. Would he would
   change!
THESEUS It appears, by his small light of discretion, that
   he is in the wane; but yet, in courtesy, in all reason, we
   must stay the time.
LYSANDER Proceed, Moon.
MOON All that I have to say is to tell you that the lanthorn
   is the moon; I, the man i' th' moon; this thornbush,
   my thornbush; and this dog, my dog.
DEMETRIUS Why, all these should be in the lanthorn, for
   all these are in the moon. But silence: here comes Thisby.
      Enter Thisby.

THISBY
   This is old Ninny's tomb. Where is my love?
LION O!   *[The Lion roars. Thisby runs off.]*   257
DEMETRIUS Well roared, Lion.
THESEUS Well run, Thisby.
HIPPOLYTA Well shone, Moon. Truly, the moon shines
   with a good grace.
         [The Lion tears Thisby's mantle, and exit.]
THESEUS Well moused, Lion.
DEMETRIUS And then came Pyramus.
LYSANDER And so the Lion vanished.
      Enter Pyramus.

PYRAMUS
   Sweet moon, I thank thee for thy sunny beams;
      I thank thee, moon, for shining now so bright;
   For, by thy gracious, golden, glittering gleams,
      I trust to take of truest Thisby sight.
            But stay: O spite!   269
            But mark, poor knight,
         What dreadful dole is here?   271
            Eyes, do you see?
            How can it be?

257 s.d. (from folio) 269 *spite* i.e. malice of fortune 271 *dole* cause of
grief, piteous thing

           O dainty duck, O dear!

              Thy mantle good,

              What, stained with blood?

277   Approach, ye Furies fell!

              O Fates, come, come,

279   Cut thread and thrum,

280   Quail, crush, conclude, and quell!

281 THESEUS This passion, and the death of a dear friend,

    would go near to make a man look sad.

283 HIPPOLYTA Beshrew my heart but I pity the man.

PYRAMUS

      O, wherefore, Nature, didst thou lions frame?

285   Since lion vile hath here deflow'red my dear;

      Which is – no, no! – which was the fairest dame

        That lived, that loved, that liked, that looked with cheer.

              Come, tears, confound,

              Out, sword, and wound

            The pap of Pyramus:

                Ay, that left pap

                Where heart doth hop.

        [Stabs himself.]

              Thus die I, thus, thus, thus.

                Now am I dead,

                Now am I fled,

              My soul is in the sky.

                Tongue, lose thy light,

                Moon, take thy flight.   [Exit Moonshine.]

              Now die, die, die, die, die.

        [Dies.]

300 DEMETRIUS No die, but an ace, for him! for he is but one.

---

277 *Furies* (invocations of the Furies were common in Senecan drama); *fell* fierce, terrible   279 *thrum* end of the warp thread left attached to the loom when the web is cut away (merely Bottom the weaver's way of saying, 'Do a complete job of it!')   280 *Quail* overpower, destroy; *quell* kill   281–82 *This . . . sad* i.e. this display of passion by itself wouldn't sadden anyone   283 *Beshrew* curse (but used lightly; cf. II, ii, 54)   285 *deflow'red* ravished   300 *ace* the one-spot on a die; *one* (quibble on 'one person' and 'unique')

LYSANDER Less than an ace, man; for he is dead, he is
  nothing.

THESEUS With the help of a surgeon he might yet
  recover, and yet prove an ass.   304

HIPPOLYTA How chance Moonshine is gone before
  Thisby comes back and finds her lover?

  [Enter Thisby.]

THESEUS She will find him by starlight. Here she comes;
  and her passion ends the play.   308

HIPPOLYTA Methinks she should not use a long one for
  such a Pyramus. I hope she will be brief.

DEMETRIUS A mote will turn the balance, which Pyramus, which Thisby, is the better: he for a man, God
  warr'nt us! – she for a woman, God bless us!   312

LYSANDER She has spied him already with those sweet
  eyes.

DEMETRIUS And thus she means, videlicet: 315

THISBY   Asleep, my love?
        What, dead, my dove?
      O Pyramus, arise!
      Speak, speak. Quite dumb?
      Dead, dead? A tomb
    Must cover thy sweet eyes.
       These lily lips,
       This cherry nose,
    These yellow cowslip cheeks,
      Are gone, are gone.
      Lovers, make moan.
    His eyes were green as leeks.   327
      O Sisters Three,   328
      Come, come to me,
    With hands as pale as milk;
      Lay them in gore,
      Since you have shore

---

304 *ass* (pun on *ace*)   **308** *passion* speech of passion   **312** *warr'nt* warrant,
i.e. protect   **315** *means* (1) laments (an Anglo-Saxon word), (2) lodges a
complaint (in a legal sense)   **327** *green* hazel   **328** *Sisters Three* the Fates

With shears his thread of silk.
Tongue, not a word.
Come, trusty sword,
336   Come, blade, my breast imbrue!
[Stabs herself.]
And farewell, friends.
Thus Thisby ends.
Adieu, adieu, adieu.
[Dies.]
[Enter Lion, Moonshine, and Wall.]

THESEUS   Moonshine and Lion are left to bury the dead.

DEMETRIUS   Ay, and Wall too.

342   LION   No, I assure you; the wall is down that parted their
fathers. Will it please you to see the epilogue, or to hear
344   a Bergomask dance between two of our company?

THESEUS   No epilogue, I pray you; for your play needs no
excuse. Never excuse, for when the players are all dead,
there need none to be blamed. Marry, if he that writ it
348   had played Pyramus and hanged himself in Thisby's garter, it would have been a fine tragedy; and so it is truly,
and very notably discharged. But, come, your Bergomask. Let your epilogue alone.
[A dance.]
352   The iron tongue of midnight hath told twelve.
Lovers, to bed; 'tis almost fairy time.   *invites all to go to bed*
I fear we shall outsleep the coming morn
355   As much as we this night have overwatched.
This palpable gross play hath well beguiled
357   The heavy gait of night. Sweet friends, to bed.
A fortnight hold we this solemnity
In nightly revels and new jollity.   *Exeunt.*

---

336 *imbrue* stain with blood   **342** *Lion* (the folio, followed by many editors,
assigns this speech to Bottom)   **344** *Bergomask dance* rustic or clownish
dance named after the peasants of Bergamo, Italy   **348–49** *hanged . . .
garter* (a proverbial phrase)   **352** *told* counted (perhaps with a quibble on
'tolled')   **355** *overwatched* stayed awake too long   **357** *heavy* drowsy

Enter Puck [with a broom].

PUCK Now the hungry lion roars,
          And the wolf behowls the moon ;
      Whilst the heavy ploughman snores,
          All with weary task fordone.   363
      Now the wasted brands do glow,
          Whilst the screech owl, screeching loud,
      Puts the wretch that lies in woe
          In remembrance of a shroud.
      Now it is the time of night
          That the graves, all gaping wide,
      Every one lets forth his sprite,   370
          In the churchway paths to glide.
      And we fairies, that do run
          By the triple Hecate's team   373
      From the presence of the sun,
          Following darkness like a dream,
      Now are frolic. Not a mouse
      Shall disturb this hallowed house.
      I am sent, with broom, before,
      To sweep the dust behind the door.   379

Enter King and Queen of Fairies, with all their Train.

OBERON Through the house give glimmering light,
            By the dead and drowsy fire ;
        Every elf and fairy sprite
            Hop as light as bird from brier ;
        And this ditty, after me,
        Sing, and dance it trippingly.

TITANIA First rehearse your song by rote,
         To each word a warbling note.

---

363 *fordone* worn out   370 *Every one* every grave; *his* its; *sprite* spirit,
ghost (cf. III, ii, 381–83)   373 *triple Hecate* Ovid's '*dea triformis*' (*Metamorphoses*, vii, 94–5, 194), Hecate in her three aspects as Luna in the sky,
Diana on earth, Proserpina in the underworld; here, both goddess of the
moon and of night; *team* i.e. of dragons (cf. III, ii, 379)   379 *behind* from
behind (Puck traditionally kept the house clean and was represented with
a broom and a candle)

389   Hand in hand, with fairy grace,
    Will we sing, and bless this place.

[Song and dance.]

OBERON Now, until the break of day,
    Through this house each fairy stray.
    To the best bride-bed will we,
    Which by us shall blessèd be;
    And the issue there create
    Ever shall be fortunate.
    So shall all the couples three
    Ever true in loving be;
    And the blots of Nature's hand
    Shall not in their issue stand.
    Never mole, harelip, nor scar,
401   Nor mark prodigious, such as are
    Despisèd in nativity,
    Shall upon their children be.
404   With this field-dew consecrate,
    Every fairy take his gait,
    And each several chamber bless,
    Through this palace, with sweet peace.
    And the owner of it blest
    Ever shall in safety rest.
    Trip away; make no stay;
    Meet me all by break of day.

Exeunt [all but Puck].

PUCK If we shadows have offended,
    Think but this, and all is mended –
    That you have but slumb'red here
    While these visions did appear.

---

389 s.d. *Song and dance* (the song referred to in ll. 384–86 may be lost, or may survive in ll. 390–411, headed as 'The Song' in the folio) **401** *mark prodigious* ominous birthmark **404** *consecrate* consecrated

And this weak and idle theme,   416
No more yielding but a dream,   417
Gentles, do not reprehend.
If you pardon, we will mend.
And, as I am an honest Puck,
If we have unearnèd luck
Now to scape the serpent's tongue,   422
We will make amends ere long;
Else the Puck a liar call.
So, good night unto you all.
Give me your hands, if we be friends,   426
And Robin shall restore amends.   *[Exit.]*

416 *idle* foolish   **417** *No more yielding but* yielding no more than   **422**
scape escape; *serpent's tongue* i.e. hissing   **426** *Give . . . hands* i.e. applaud

APPENDIX:
SUPPLEMENTARY NOTE ON
THE TEXT

The first quarto, printed in 1600, is the authoritative text of the play, although it contains a number of errors difficult to emend. Judging from the sparse stage directions, the inconsistent speech-prefixes (such as both *Puck* and *Robin, Bottom* and *Clown*), the careless assignment of minor parts, many old-fashioned spellings, and other small signs, the text was very probably set up from Shakespeare's own working manuscript of the play rather than from a clean copy prepared for use in the theatre. Certain irregularities of the 1600 text, moreover, especially the mislining of passages of verse in the last scene (including Theseus' famous speech on the madman, the lover, and the poet), would seem to indicate that Shakespeare had made some marginal additions; and certain other features of the play, notably the inconsistencies in the time scheme, may have arisen from a more extensive revision. The duration of the action can be stretched, at most, to three days, not to the four days and four nights announced by Hippolyta as the interval until her wedding; and the moon, not expected to be new until that day, shines on the night the lovers elope and the actors rehearse, and is everywhere present in the poetry. But whether these and other anomalies all imply revision and whether, if they do, the revising was simply part of the process of composition or a more thorough job done after an interval for a particular occasion, there is no means of deciding. Professor J. Dover Wilson has suggested as such an occasion the wedding in 1598 of the Earl of Southampton to Elizabeth Vernon.

The first quarto was reprinted in 1619 in a second quarto falsely dated 1600; the reprint contained many minor corrections, but also many new errors, and many sophistications of spelling and punctuation. This second quarto was in turn reprinted, with a continuation of its errors and with the introduction of a number of "improved" readings carrying the text further away from Shakespeare, in the folio of 1623. The 1619 quarto used as copy for the folio printers, however, must have had transferred to it a number of stage directions, some corrected speech-prefixes, and some changed assignments of minor parts from a theatrical manuscript, presumably one in use by the company at that date. About half a dozen new readings for which a printer can hardly have been responsible must have come from the theatrical manuscript. Several of these are certainly wrong; the others (see list of emendations, III, ii, 19, 220; V, i, 189, 204) may or may not have been what Shakespeare wrote.

The division into acts introduced in the folio may have come from the theatrical manuscript, and if so reflects a change in the style of production; it may, however, have been only editorial, since it does great damage to the management of the scenes. In the original quarto text (which is undivided into acts and in which the scenes are not numbered) there are only seven scenes, counting a clear stage as a change of scene. Two scenes outside the wood begin the play (the first by implication of the text at the court of Theseus; the second, a meeting of the "mechanicals," not located by the text in any particular place), and two scenes outside (the same as the first two, in reverse order) end it. All the action in between (II, i through IV, i in the editorial numbering) is in the wood, and is nearly continuous, with the stage clear only twice (before II, ii and before III, ii). Titania remains asleep on the stage where the folio makes a break with Act III, and the lovers are so asleep where it makes a break with Act IV. The folio direction at the end of Act III, "They sleepe all the Act," is usually taken to mean "all the act-interval," but may mean "during the following act" (through IV, i, 137); in either case, it is consequent upon the division into acts and tends to support, though it does not prove, the theory that the division had been made for presentation.

The following are the only readings in the present edition departing materially from the text of the first quarto. Corrections of simple literal errors, punctuation, and mislineation of verse are not noted unless they affect the sense. After each reading, in italics, the corresponding text actually appearing in the quartos and folio is given in roman. When the reading is from the second quarto or the folio, the fact is indicated; otherwise it is an emendation, usually one suggested quite early in the history of Shakespearean scholarship.

I, i, 4 *wanes* (Q2, F) waues (Q1)   10 *New-bent* Now bent (QQ, F)
19 s.d. *omitting* '*Helena*' (F) *including* '*Helena*' (QQ)   24 *Stand
forth, Demetrius* printed as s.d. (QQ, F)   26 *Stand forth, Lysander* printed as s.d. (QQ, F)   136 *low* loue (QQ, F)   187 *Yours
would* Your words (QQ, F)   191 *I'ld* ile (Q1) Ile (Q2, F)   216
sweet sweld (QQ, F)   219 *stranger companies* strange companions
(QQ, F)

I, ii, 24 *rest. Yet* rest yet (QQ, F)   25–26 *split.* / '*The* split the (QQ, F)

II, i, 69 *steep* (Q2, F 'steepe') steppe (Q1)   79 *Aegles* Eagles (QQ, F)
109 *thin* chinne (QQ, F)   158 *by the* (F) by (QQ)   190 *slay . . .
slayeth* stay . . . stayeth (QQ, F)   201 *nor I* (F) not I (QQ)

II, ii, 39 *Be't* Bet it (Q1) Be it (Q2, F)   43 *good* (Q2, F) god (Q1)   47
is (Q2, F) it (Q1)

III, i, 27 *yourselves* (F) your selfe (QQ)   49 *Bottom* (Q2, F 'Bot.')
Cet. (Q1)   61 *and let* or let (QQ, F)   74 *Odorous, odorous*
Odours, odorous (QQ) Odours, odours (F)   79 *Puck* (F) Quin.
(QQ)   148–49 *Peaseblossom, etc.* Fairies. Readie : and I, and I,
and I. Where shall we goe ? (QQ, F)   161–64 *Peaseblossom, etc.*
1. Fai. Haile mortall, haile. / 2. Fai. Haile. / 3. Fai. Haile. (QQ, F)
181 *you of more* you more (QQ, F)

III, ii, 19 *mimic* (F 'Mimmick') minnick (Q1) Minnock (Q2)   80
part I so part I (QQ, F)   85 *sleep* slippe (Q1) slip (Q2, F)   213
first, like first life (QQ, F)   220 *passionate* (F) omitted (QQ)
237 *Ay, do. Perseuer* I doe. Perseuer (Q1) I, do, perseuer (Q2, F)
250 *prayers* praise (QQ, F)   257 *No, no, you'll* No, no : heele (Q1)
No, no, hee'l (Q2) No, no, Sir (F)   299 *gentlemen* (Q2, F) gentleman (Q1)   406 *Speak! In some bush?* Speake in some bush.
(QQ, F)   451 *To your* your (QQ, F)

IV, i, 40 *all ways* alwaies (QQ, F)   41 *woodbine . . . honeysuckle*
woodbine, . . . Honisuckle, (QQ, F)   65 *That, he* That hee, (Q1)
That he (Q2, F)   72 *o'er* or (QQ, F)   81 *sleep of all these five*
sleep : of all these, fine (QQ, F)   116 *Seemed* Seeme (QQ, F)   127
this is (Q2, F) this (Q1)   132 *rite* right (QQ, F)   171 *saw* see (QQ,
F)   198 *let us* (Q2, F) lets (Q1)   205 *to expound* (Q2, F) expound
(Q1)   207 *a patched* (F) patcht a (QQ)   214 *our play* a Play
(QQ, F)

IV, ii, s.d. *Enter . . . Starveling* Enter Quince, Flute, Thisby and
the rabble (QQ) Enter Quince, Flute, Thisbie, Snout, and
Staruveling (F)   3 *Starveling* (F 'Staru.') Flut. (QQ)   5, 9, 13, 18
Flute Thys. *or* This. (QQ, F)

V, i, 34 *our* (F) Or (Q1) or (Q2)   155 *Snout* (F) Flute (QQ)   189 *up in thee* (F) now againe (QQ)   192 *My love! thou art my love,* My loue thou art, my loue (QQ, F)   204 *mural down* Moon vsed (QQ) morall downe (F)   215 *beasts in, a* beasts, in a (QQ, F)   267 *gleams* beames (QQ, F)   305–06 *gone before Thisby* gone before? Thisby (QQ, F)   311 *mote* moth (QQ, F)   360 *lion* Lyons (QQ, F)   361 *behowls* beholds (Q, F)   408–09 these two lines transposed (QQ, F)

The Complete Pelican

SHAKESPEARE

To fill the need for a convenient and authoritative one-volume edition, the thirty-eight books in the Pelican series have been brought together.

THE COMPLETE PELICAN SHAKESPEARE includes all the material contained in the separate volumes, together with a 50,000-word General Introduction and full bibliographies. It contains the first nineteen pages of the First Folio in reduced facsimile, five new drawings, and illustrated endpapers.

$9\frac{3}{4} \times 7\frac{3}{16}$ inches, 1520 pages
Trade Edition cloth-bound, in jacket and slipcase
Text Edition cloth-bound

PENGUIN SHAKESPEARE LIBRARY

General Editor: Professor T. J. B. Spencer
Director of the Shakespeare Institute, University of Birmingham

A new series of reprints of critical works, source-books, and other aids to the understanding of Shakespeare

PELICAN GUIDE TO ENGLISH
LITERATURE

Edited by Boris Ford
Dean of the School of Educational Studies, University of Sussex

Volume 2 contains detailed essays on the plays of Shakespeare, and on individual dramatists, poets, and prose writers – Marlowe, Ben Jonson, Bacon, etc.

A SHAKESPEARE COMPANION

F. E. Halliday

A simple and handy index to all aspects of Shakespearean lore over four centuries.

Three Comedies – Ben Jonson
    Volpone, The Alchemist, Bartholomew Fair

Three Elizabethan Domestic Tragedies
    Arden of Faversham
    A Yorkshire Tragedy
    A Woman Killed with Kindness – Thomas Heywood

Three Jacobean Tragedies
    The Changeling – Thomas Middleton
    The Revenger's Tragedy – Cyril Tourneur
    The White Devil – John Webster

Three Restoration Comedies
    Love for Love – William Congreve
    The Man of Mode – George Etherege
    The Country Wife – William Wycherley

Also works by Jane Austen, Beckford, Charlotte and Emily Brontë, Bunyan, Samuel Butler, Cobbett, Wilkie Collins, Defoe, Dickens, George Eliot, Fielding, Gissing, Samuel Johnson, Malory, Melville, Meredith, Peacock, Poe, Mary Shelley, Smollett, Sterne, Swift, Thackeray, Trollope, Mark Twain, and Walpole.

Other volumes in preparation

PLAYS BY BERNARD SHAW

Androcles and the Lion

The Apple Cart

Arms and the Man

Back to Methuselah

Caesar and Cleopatra

Candida

The Devil's Disciple

The Doctor's Dilemma

Major Barbara

Man and Superman

The Millionairess

Plays Unpleasant

Pygmalion

Saint Joan

Seven One-Act Plays

Selected One-Act Plays, Volumes 1 and 2